Diamond Beauty

God's Beauty Plan for Women

Dona Moriarty

DIAMOND BEAUTY – GOD'S BEAUTY PLAN FOR WOMEN

Copyright © 2023 by Dona Moriarty

Published by Kingdom Books Publishing, 2023

All rights reserved. No part of this publication may be reproduced, distributed, transmitted, or stored in a retrieval system, in any form or by any means, without permission in writing from the publisher, except in the case of brief quotations embodied in critical reviews and certain other non-commercial uses. For information, address the publisher at Kingdom Books LLC, P.O. Box 481, Carlsbad, CA 92018

Kingdom Books LLC books may be purchased for education, business, or sales promotional use. For information, please e-mail info@kingdombookspublishing.com with the subject Special Markets

ISBN: 979-8-9866874-6-9

ISBN: 979-8-9866874-7-6

Cover Designed by: David Ewing at Heave Ho Creative

Scripture taken from the New King James Version®. Copyright © 1982 by Thomas Nelson. Used by permission. All rights reserved. Scripture quotations marked MSG are taken from The Message, copyright © 1993, 2002, 2018 by Eugene H. Peterson. Used by permission of NavPress. All rights reserved. Represented by Tyndale House Publishers. Scripture quotations marked (NLT) are taken from the Holy Bible, New Living Translation, copyright ©1996, 2004, 2015 by Tyndale House Foundation. Used by permission of Tyndale House Publishers, Carol Stream, Illinois 60188. All rights reserved. Scripture quotations taken from the Amplified® Bible (AMP), Copyright © 2015 by The Lockman Foundation. Used by permission. lockman.org. Scripture quotations marked (NIV) are taken from the Holy Bible, New International Version®, NIV®. Copyright © 1973, 1978, 1984, 2011 by Biblica, Inc.™ Used by permission of Zondervan. All rights reserved worldwide. www.zondervan.comThe "NIV" and "New International Version" are trademarks registered in the United States Patent and Trademark Office by Biblica, Inc.™

This book is dedicated to every woman who reads it because you are passionate to learn how to reflect God's glory. May the Holy Spirit speak to you in a unique way.

Table of Contents

Introduction 1

PART I: THE BEAUTY PLAN - SALVATION 7

Chapter 1: God Wants You to be Beautiful 9

Chapter 2: God's Beauty Framework 27

Chapter 3: Salvation: God's Beauty Process 55

Chapter 4: How the Devil Has Twisted God's Plan 91

PART II: THE BEAUTY TREATMENTS 109

Chapter 5: The Water Treatments 111

Chapter 6: The Fires of Sanctification 131

Chapter 7: The Optimal Diet 155

Chapter 8: A Royal Wardrobe 181

Conclusion 199

REFLECTION QUESTIONS 201

Introduction

So here you are—curious enough to crack open these pages. They tell me someone decides if they want to read a book halfway down the first page, so I am going to cut right to the chase and tell you what God showed me when I started to wonder what God thought about the issue of beauty for His daughters. Women are wired with a desire to feel beautiful. As a marriage and family therapist, I have had a lot of women confess how secretly insecure they are with their beauty. When I began to research this, it surprised me that "only four percent of women around the world consider themselves beautiful. Believe it or not, this is a doubled increase from just two percent in 2004. Also, 80 percent of women agree that every woman has something about her that is beautiful, but do not see their own beauty."[1] I realized God put a deposit into every woman that is in some way beautiful. Most of us can recognize it in each other. It's not a matter of having beauty, it's a matter of recognizing and developing it in ourselves. This being the case, I asked God how He wanted that to happen in each woman's life.

When we look at our culture, there are some shocking statistics of where we have ended up in the pursuit of beauty by the world's standards:

- In the United States alone about 10 million women suffer from eating disorders. As the mother of 4 daughters, one of whom suffered through this terrible disorder, this is an issue very close to my heart. We will dive into this later in the book.
- A whopping 80% of women report being dissatisfied with their appearance.[2]
- A total of 7 billion dollars are spent a year on cosmetics.[3] This number continues to escalate as women are taking more and more drastic measures to alter their appearances. Newsweek reports that by the time a 10 year old is 50, she'll have spent nearly $300,000 on just her hair and face.[4]
- As a result of reality TV makeovers, ads of airbrushed Victoria Secret models, and the

internet, (with its deluge of celebrity fashion shots, make-up and grooming tips), teenagers spend $100 million per month on beauty products, and the trend is getting younger. It is estimated that 8-12 year olds spend $40 million per month on beauty products.[5]

- Cosmetic surgery performed on those 18 or younger has nearly doubled in the past decade, and 69% of young people are in favor of it.[6]
- Psychologists believe these ever harder to achieve beauty standards have a negative impact on a girl's self-esteem. The average 11-16 year old sees some 500 advertisements a day usually of altered, perfected model images, reports a University of Minnesota study, and viewing those images for only 1-3 minutes has a negative impact on girls.[7]

While I prayed, God laid out two specific Bible passages that address His beauty plan for women. The first was Ezekiel 16: 4-14. This is God speaking to His Bride (the church—aka you and me in present day and Israel in the Old Testament). In the passage, which we will discuss more fully throughout the book, God lays out how once we are His, He specifically plans for us to become an amazing beauty. We are called to *reflect Him and carry His glory.* That, my friend, is what this book is about: understanding the spiritual beautification process God wants to apply to you so you can fully embrace it, reflect His glory, and be an example of splendor because you are His daughter.

The meaning of glory in Hebrew is literally "weightiness" (*chabod* or *kabowd*, Strong's # 3519), as in something that is substantial, full of honor, splendor, power, magnificence, dignity, and excellence. As women in our time are fighting more than ever for the recognition of their worth and value, it has been God's plan all along to endow His daughters with power, dignity and honor. He wants us to shine in strength. In that respect, feminism has the right goal, but the method of getting there is flawed. Our efforts to attain freedom from one type of "bondage" should never lead to another type of bondage. Through walking in God's truth, we get real freedom (see John 8:31-32), so we can achieve the "liberation" our sisters strived for.

God wants to give every woman *diamond* beauty. He specifically whispered the word diamond into my mind. "Why diamonds?" I wondered. Despite wearing my diamond wedding band for almost 40 years, I was never a big jewelry girl, so I was ignorant about diamonds and their qualities. I learned diamonds are the most brilliant and valuable gems in the world. They are purchased more than all other gems put together.[8] In addition to their beauty, they possess unbreakable strength—the strongest material in the world. The Greeks called a diamond *adamas*, which means unmovable, indestructible. They are also a symbol of undying love. Once formed, their brilliance, strength and value are unchanging. They are priceless. How amazing. *God's goal is to make His daughters the most valuable, desired and strong symbol of His undying love.* His plans for us, as women, go way beyond our desires and dreams (see Ephesians 3:20). So how do we develop diamond beauty?

That brings me to the second Bible passage God showed me. Psalm 103:1-5 lays out the process of transformation which we will look at in depth in chapter 3. In this passage, David explains the five benefits, or good things God does for us as we walk with Him.

> "He forgives all my sins and heals all my diseases. He redeems me from death and crowns me with love and tender mercies. He fills my life with good things. My youth is renewed like the eagle's!"(Psalm 103:1-5 NLT)

The Lord begins to beautify us the day we begin to walk in His salvation. The beauty plan is the 5-point process David lays out in this Psalm—these are the "benefits" of salvation that transform us day by day.

The rest of this book is an in-depth study of what that looks like, including the spiritual beauty treatments for attaining a beauty that goes beyond appearances to the core of transforming you into the beautiful woman He created. I am praying as I write this that you will be inspired by the Holy Spirit, learning how to become a woman who is a reflection of *His* glory, a woman of unfading diamond quality beauty.

Part I:
The Beauty Plan – Salvation

Chapter 1
God Wants You to be Beautiful

Why does God care about beauty in the first place? Because God has chosen you (and if you are reading this, you probably responded to His invitation), so you are His in every way. In your relationship with Him as God the Father, you are His daughter. As Jesus' reason for coming to the earth, you are His bride. In your relationship with the Holy Spirit, you are His dwelling place, the representation of Him everywhere you go in the world. He is designing you to be a radiant reflection of Him in every aspect as Father, Son and Holy Spirit. Here are some points to ponder about why making you a diamond beauty is a certainty of His plan, so you can settle it in your heart:

His creation demonstrates His excellence as a designer and artist

We are his workmanship (Ephesians 2:10). "Workmanship" is the word *poiema* (Strong's #4161) from which poem and poetry are derived. It actually means a design that has been produced by an artisan. God is the master craftsman, the artisan, that has designed and created each one of us to be His works of art. A master artist produces beautiful works of art, but in order for a work of art to retain its value, it has to be an original, one of a kind. That is why God takes the time to create our hearts, as well as our faces and bodies, *individually*. If you try to be an imitation of someone else, then you are a copy, a "knock-off." That seriously limits your ability to be what God designed you to be, and it dims the qualities that make you so special. The enemy of our soul would like for you to be satisfied imitating the images of someone else so you never transform into the work of art God has made *only you to be*. Trust the Master to keep putting His own special, personal touch on you. You were created to be an original.

He has made you as an individual physically and spiritually. He anoints you and has the Holy Spirit come to you as an individual. Your relationship with Him, if you want a close one, is walked out individually. Hanging out with someone in a group setting brings a certain level of familiarity (in this case church, small groups, etc.), but it's the one-on-one time that makes us really close to someone. Relationship with God is one-on-one in both directions. You are His and He is yours in a unique way.

Most people are aware every person has a unique fingerprint, but did you know research reveals every person responds to God differently? When MRI studies were done while people were asked to think about God, no two brains responded exactly the same way. Each person's brain functioned differently as they thought about Him.[9] You have a special connection that no one else can have with Him. God planned it that way because you are uniquely His "poiema". If you are a mom, you know exactly what I mean. No matter how many kids you have, each one is special to you, and each relationship is a little different. There might be some similarities, but one child cannot take another's place in your life or heart. No one is able to take your place with God and He intentionally created it that way.

Every tiny detail of who you are is important to God because He is the King of detail. David was overwhelmed when the understanding of that hit him. He expressed it in Psalm 139. In verses 13-18 David writes how God planned every detail of our bodies and lives from conception to our last day:

"For You formed my inward parts; You covered me in my mother's womb. I will praise You, for I am fearfully and wonderfully made...*skillfully wrought* in the lowest parts of the earth. Your eyes saw my substance, being yet unformed."(Psalm 139:13-18 NKJ)

I started off my education at FIT, the Fashion Institute of Technology, in New York City and while I was there, I had a front row seat to how meticulously good designers pore over the particulars of their work. Whether it's textures, colors, lines, or shapes, designers take great pain and pleasure in creating specific things that express who they are and bring joy to others. This is exactly what God did, and is doing, when creating and transforming you. God is the first, most brilliant designer that ever existed.

At the risk of sounding too corny, have you ever been to a majestic mountain feeling tiny and insignificant? Have you ever looked at a flower really closely and marveled at the intensity of the color and how delicate and soft the petals are? Have you ever seen fall foliage at its peak and felt awed? Or maybe sat by turquoise water at a beach and marveled that it could be real? Or at a clear night sky full of brilliant stars? It is difficult to articulate our amazement because words never do justice in those moments when the beauty of creation hits you. David declares just that:

"When I consider Your heavens, the work of Your fingers, the moon and the stars, which You have ordained, what is man that You are mindful of him... And *You have crowned him with glory and honor.*" (Psa. 8:3-5)

When you think about how beautiful God made the world and the endless variety of plants, animals and stars—even the intricacy of a tiny snowflake—it is overwhelming to think that *you* (yes, I mean *you*) are the crown of all of creation! Crazy, isn't it? Yet that is what God revealed to David who expressed it in Psalm 8, specifically in verse 5: "You have made them a little lower than the angels and crowned them with glory and honor." The word honor, translated from *hadar* (Strong's #1926) literally means that which is full of "splendor, honor, glory, adornment, magnificence and beauty." I am in awe when I consider that this is the description of who God made us to be. You are created to be God's work of art and as you function in that unique way, you are truly beautiful.

We often see that other women have beauty in some way, but can't see it in ourselves. Embracing your uniqueness, being determined not to try to be a knock-off of someone else, will make it much easier to see your own beauty. Take a moment and just embrace the thought that you are truly unique and irreplaceable.

Since Jesus sent the Holy Spirit, we are now His dwelling place which means we are beautiful.

Psalm 84:1 states, "How lovely are Your dwellings, O Lord of hosts!"

When the implication of what this verse meant hit me, I could not stop smiling. God's dwelling places are beautiful to Him. Because He dwells in me, I am lovely. Have you ever read the chapters of how He wanted the tabernacle set up in the Old Testament? Exodus, Leviticus, Numbers, and Deuteronomy all record the way God wanted it to look down to the last thread on the high priest's vest! In Exodus 28:2, the Lord expresses His purpose for the priestly garments to be that way simply for "glory and for beauty." How much more important are we, His daughters, than the vests of the Old Testament priests?

Before Jesus came, God did not dwell in His people, even though He dwelt *with* them. His glory was expressed visibly in His tabernacle and by the priests who ministered to Him. After Jesus came, and sacrificed Himself for us on the cross, we were completely reconciled to Him and able to have God live right in us. No more separations, except by our own choice.

In 1 Corinthians 3:16 Paul says, "Do you not know you are the temple of God, and that the spirit of God dwells *in* you?" We are now his lovely dwelling place! He wants us to be the most visible expression of His beauty to the world.

I want to take a little pause here because I can hear some of you saying to yourself, 'but I do not feel that way. That sounds nice, but I do not feel beautiful or lovely." I get it because I have walked through it, so let's examine the "why" of not feeling lovely for a minute. Is it because you have put what you "should" look like in your mind above God's design for you? Is it maybe because you have bought the world's lie that there is a certain beauty standard—and it's usually the one you can't achieve? Often, we say the right thing out loud, (some version of "everyone is beautiful in their own way") but inside, you might be thinking, "but I want to be beautiful like this."

Isaiah 45:8-10 reveals God's frustration when the pot says to the potter, "why have You made me like this?" Basically, the pot is saying, "You are doing a bad job because this isn't the way I would have chosen to be." You see, God is forming us to be a vessel that is perfect for what He is going to use us to do (see Ephesians 2:10). A vessel does not have the capacity to fully understand it's purpose as a potter is forming it.

Jesus told the tired people following Him that His yoke was easy and His burden was light in Matthew 11:30. That word easy, in this context, means "useful, comfortable, suitable, pleasant" (Strong's #5543). When you trust God to form and transform you into His vessel, it will not be an exhausting burden that leaves you uncomfortable. When I think of all the different "vessels" I have around me, I value and love the ones that are formed to do their job excellently. My crockpot needs to work very differently than my washing machine. It needs to be shaped very differently. I love each of them for what they do in my life! That may sound silly, but we have a purpose that we are uniquely called to fulfill. If my crockpot spent its days refusing to cook yummy dinners because it wished it looked and functioned like a washing machine, it would be useless not to mention annoying. It would lose all its value and be discarded. Many women have allowed their value to be diminished because they bemoan they are skinny rather than curvy, or curvy rather than skinny, or have a stomach that is shaped differently or smaller breasts, rather than embracing each feature as uniqueness (see Proverbs 14:1).

Thankfully, God is so patient as He continues to gently mold us into the specific vessel He intends for us to be. He will never discard us, but He wants us to look beyond the physical to the higher calling we have in Him. He does not want us to confuse physical attractiveness with the real beauty that will make us shine from the inside out which we will discuss in the next chapter in depth.

"But I still feel bad about my body or nose or weight," you might say. I have a suggestion to help you walk in freedom. Rather than accusing the Master Creator with not making you the way you want, have a serious conversation with Him about your struggle, asking to see what He sees. Ask Him to transform your understanding rather than your physical attributes (see Romans 12:1-2). Lay out a strategy to reach your goals *with* Him and submit it to His loving hand. He created your heart, and

He understands all your feelings and desires (see Psalm 33:15). He also wants to give you the desires of your heart as you delight yourself in Him (see Psalm 37:4). For example, tell Him you want a nose job, and ask Him to direct your steps so it works out well, or give Him permission to change your heart if it is not really going to make you feel better about yourself. Ask Him to get to the root of the insecurity, as you work on presenting your best self. Paul says that everything is lawful, but not everything is good for us.

In my case, I decided after many years of hating the huge stretch marks and skin hanging around my middle after my 5 kids, that I would get a tummy tuck which turned into a full mommy makeover when I was in my 40s. My plastic surgeon told me women will not be happier with themselves if they are looking for surgery to solve their emotional and insecurity struggles. He had been doing reconstructive surgery for years and had seen women's discontent over and over. He was right in my case. Even though it was a blessing, I had plenty of moments of insecurity about myself after my mommy makeover. Even though I finally had a belly button again, it was not the answer to my deep-down insecurities.

I want to encourage you to make a decision to trust Him with your body, mind, and heart. As a therapist, I have listened to unhappy, beautiful women complain about their perceived imperfections. I have also seen others embrace their identity in Christ, choosing to "feed" on what He says about His daughters, and letting Him transform and mold them into a beautiful, confident work of art, as they trusted His shaping process.

As He dwells in you, and shapes you, you are His lovely dwelling place. Pray for a revelation of this identity in your heart, as you choose to embrace that concept. Just as you can see the beauty (and potential of beauty) in other women, ask Him to help you see it in yourself!

> We are His daughters— and that means we are to reflect Him and bear the family resemblance.

God as our heavenly Father wants us to look like Him. When we walk into a room, He wants others to see Him in us. I used to be the spitting image of my dad as a little girl. My mom would laugh and say my dad would never be able to claim I was not his child. All people would have to do is take one look at me, and they would know we were related. We had the same eyes, the same nose, and the same round face—even the same chubby toes.

Once you give your heart to the Lord, you become His child. As you spend time with Him, you begin to look more and more like Him. Jesus told the disciples in John 14:9-10, that anyone who has seen Him, has seen the Father: "He who has seen Me has seen the Father...The words that I speak to you I do not speak on My own authority; but the Father who dwells in Me does the works." Everything Jesus did reflected the Father. To know one was to know the other.

If your dad was not there for you and that is a hard concept, consider the following:

In Isaiah 49: 15-16 the Lord gently says:

"Can a woman forget her nursing child, and not have compassion on the son of her womb? Surely they may forget, yet I will not forget you. See, I have inscribed you on the palms of My hands..."

When Jesus looks at His nail scarred hands, He thinks of you—someone He died for! He could never forget you. His love for you is literally inscribed on His hands for all of eternity because of the cross—the place where He gave everything He had for you. He did this to close any separation between you and the Father, so He could be with you and by His Spirit dwell in you forever.

Psalm 27:10 says, "When my father and mother forsake me, then the Lord will take care of me."

God, your Father, will take care of you and never leave you or abandon you. Never ever, even if for some reason your own natural parents do (or have). Stop and take a moment to let this truth sink deep into the recesses of your heart. Once you give your heart to the Lord and walk with Him, you are *never* alone again. The very God of the universe lives in you!

It is God's pleasure as your dad to give you the heritage that belongs to you as His beloved daughter. Embrace His complete faithfulness, become "at home" in His love, and continue to grow in the family resemblance.

We are Jesus' bride—and a woman eventually reflects her husband's care and love spiritually, emotionally and physically.

Ephesians 5:25-28 in the Message translation puts it so beautifully:

"Husbands, go all out in your love for your wives, exactly as Christ did for the church—a love marked by giving, not getting. Christ's love makes the church whole. *His words evoke her beauty. Everything He does and says is designed to bring the best out of her*, dressing her in dazzling white silk, radiant with holiness. And that is how husbands ought to love their wives."

Whether you are married or single, and no matter what any other man in your life has done or said, God's plan for you is to become radiant with His glory as *His* bride. Christ gave Himself for you with everything He had down to His very last breath on the cross. The purpose of what He did was to make a way to "bring the best out in you." Making us radiant is His main motivation as our heavenly husband to present to Himself a perfect bride.

In Ezekiel 16, Ezekiel paints a touching picture of God's love for His bride, (aka you and me, just in case you forgot!):

4-5 "'On the day you were born your umbilical cord was not cut, you weren't bathed and cleaned up, you weren't rubbed with salt, you weren't wrapped in a baby blanket. No one cared a fig for you. No one did one thing to care for you tenderly in these ways. You were thrown out into a vacant lot and left there, dirty and unwashed— a newborn nobody wanted.

6-7 "'And then I came by. I saw you all miserable and bloody. Yes, I said to you, lying there helpless and filthy, "Live! Grow up like a plant in the field!" And you did. You grew up. You grew tall and matured as a woman, full-breasted, with flowing hair. But you were naked and vulnerable, fragile and exposed.

8-14 "'I came by again and saw you, saw that you were ready for love and a lover. I took care of you, dressed you and protected you. I promised you my love and entered the covenant of marriage with you. I, God, the Master, gave my word. You became mine. I gave you a good bath, washing off all that old blood, and anointed you with aromatic oils. I dressed you in a colorful gown and put leather sandals on your feet. I gave you linen blouses and a fashionable wardrobe of expensive clothing. I adorned you with jewelry: I placed bracelets on your wrists, fitted you out with a necklace, emerald rings, sapphire earrings, and a diamond tiara. You were provided with everything precious and beautiful: with exquisite clothes and elegant food, garnished with honey and oil. You were absolutely stunning. You were a queen! You became world-famous, a legendary beauty brought to perfection by my adornments. Decree of God, the Master."

He describes an unloved child, someone who the world didn't acknowledge or even want. "No eye pitied you...you were abhorred on the day you were born."(v. 4,

5) This was not about someone who was born as the beautiful, adored darling of her family or society. She was not destined for love or a modeling career. Ezekiel describes a forsaken, rejected child no one was willing to care for. She was left in an open field, abandoned to die. Then God (v. 6, 7) gently takes this child, encourages her to live, and makes her thrive like a plant until she matures into young womanhood. He sees she is "naked and vulnerable, fragile and exposed." He wants to protect her and make sure she becomes everything she is capable of being. He chooses to "spread His wing over her," or as the Message Bible explains in v. 8, "I promised you my love and entered the covenant of marriage with you. I, God, the Master, gave my word. You became mine." As the Lord, her husband, cherishes her, and provides her "with everything precious and beautiful," (v. 9-14), she "became world-famous, a legendary beauty brought to perfection by my adornments. Decree of God, the Master" (v. 14). This is a glorious picture of what God does as He transforms us to reflect His glory and image. We become beautiful because of *what He does*, not because of what we are born with.

Another thing the Lord wants you to realize is that because Jesus is your beloved and you are His (Song of Sololmon 6:3), He sees you through loving eyes as "fairest among women"(S of S 1:8) And He sees you that way *now*. The Song of Solomon is God's love song to His Bride, the Shulamite, expressing the beauty that He is captivated by and the passionate way He loves her *immediately*. God always sees us in our fulfilled potential because He looks at us through true love's eyes which means He "believes all things and hopes all things" (see 1 Corinthians 13:7), seeing the best in us. He sees us with our potential realized. I want to think of and see myself like He sees me. Don't you?

Because of His love, the Shulamite is transformed in how she feels about and sees herself. In the beginning, she is ashamed of her appearance telling Him "do not look upon me" (1:6). She explains she hasn't taken care of her "own vineyard" while she was busy tending to the business life forced on her. Have you ever bemoaned the life or body that was forced on you? Maybe you feel ashamed because you think you were conceived at the shallow end of the gene pool. Maybe you have been hurt, abused, or told you were ugly and will never be desired. Maybe you have experienced illness or addictions that have taken a toll on your body and emotional strength. But she decides to take a chance on letting go of her loneliness, and insecurity. She left the place of an outcast (S of S1:7), no longer "veiling herself", or hiding. That's a choice only we can make for ourselves. She is so much like us, seeing herself through her fears and perceived deficits which make her hesitant to become close to God and others and to trust Him, but taking the risk brought her great reward.

Paul said "Brethren (sisteren)I do not count myself to have apprehended, but one thing I do....I press toward the goal of the upward call of God in Jesus Christ." (Phil. 3:13-14 NKJ) The image of pressing that Paul references is to strain every muscle like a runner does to cross the finish line. Let's press on with understanding of our beauty and self-worth, until we attain every ounce of the transformation process God has for us. Shed off the old mindset that you can only be happy if you look a certain way. Let the Master Artist and Designer transform you and let's attain His diamond beauty together.

Now that you understand it is your destiny to be beautiful, let's take a look at His plan for how to bring out the best in you. His plan leads to freedom and confidence that actually grows as you age. That is something worth investing in even more than the new miracle moisturizer on the store shelf.

Chapter 2
God's Beauty Framework

Most women focus on how to beautify themselves on the outside. Physical beauty holds the promise of popularity, confidence, and the admiring attention of others. God wants us to shine physically, but when it's the *primary* goal, research shows it has a negative result.

All this money, time, and energy devoted to becoming physically beautiful is backfiring, and making us *more* dissatisfied at younger and younger ages, because it is opposite of the way God designed us to grow and thrive to become beautiful. The foundation of diamond beauty is God's Inside-Out Plan: God made us spirit, soul and body and He wants us to grow from our inside foundation (our spirit), to our thoughts and emotions (our soul), and lastly to the outside (our body). When the inside is strong and healthy, it will eventually become evident on the outside like the fruit on a tree. Fruit is a natural extension of what has been going on inside of the tree all year long. Your physical beauty will be a natural extension of the beauty in your spirit and soul. As you allow God to mature you and work in your heart, your perception and confidence of your value will be shaped by your relationship with Him and His Word, rather than the constant stream of external beauty messages. Let's look at how your spirit, soul and body each play a role in lasting diamond quality beauty.

Spirit Strength

There are two reasons why your spirit is top priority to God. The first is that your spirit is the eternal part of you. The second is because a close relationship with you is what He values most. God is spirit and true connection with Him happens by His Spirit to your spirit. God can only reveal the deep things about Himself to you through His Spirit. It is in this place where you build an intimate relationship with Him. Because your spirit gets renewed day by day and is eternal, Peter explains to us that the beauty we are developing in our spirit is "incorruptible"—it won't ever dissolve or decay and is very precious in the sight of God (1 Peter 3:4). The spirit connection is valuable because it is your limitless source of true confidence, strength, and joy.

Paul explains why the spirit is important in I Corinthians 2:12-16, NIV:

"However, as it is written: "What we have received is not the spirit of the world, but the Spirit who is from God, so that we may understand what God has freely given us...*The person without the Spirit does not accept the things that come from the Spirit of God but considers them foolishness, and cannot understand them because they are discerned only through the Spirit.*"

This is why Jesus told Nicodemus a man cannot enter the kingdom of heaven unless he is born again (John 3:5). A spiritual birth occurs when you repent and make Jesus your Lord. Salvation is based on having a relationship with God and asking Him to come dwell in you by the Holy Spirit. As with all relationships, you have to actively seek it. You have to ask God for His Spirit. "If you then, being evil, know how to give good gifts to your children, how much more will your heavenly Father *give the Holy Spirit to those who ask Him!*" (Luke 11:13; Matthew 7:11; Acts 1:5, 2:4, 8:17, 9:17, 10:44-45, 19:1-6).

Note: Understanding The Baptism of the Holy Spirit

For those of you that want more understanding on this topic, I have an excellent resource that looks at the subject in depth: https://theholyspirit.com/study-series/baptism-in-the-holy-spirit/. Because of the controversial nature of whether there is a separate reception of the Holy Spirit after initially accepting Jesus as your Lord, please read: Acts 1:5, 2:4, 8:14-17, 9:17-18,10:44-45, 19:1-6.

Having the Spirit living in us, the only one who knows the thoughts and deep things of God, as we read above (I Cor.2:11), is the way God is present with us today. The Spirit is literally the one who took over for Jesus when He ascended back to the Father, empowering us to live for God and understand His thoughts and ways. Without Him, it is like asking a blind man to appreciate a Picasso. He cannot begin to comprehend it because he doesn't possess the ability to see. The Spirit in us opens our spiritual eyes to see and understand God.

Why does this matter in building diamond beauty? Building spirit strength gives you a solid foundation when the outside storms of self-esteem and body dissatisfaction blow and try to knock you down. So much can happen to us during the course of our lives that we do not expect, making us feel insecure. It is very difficult to rise above that if we do not have a spiritual framework from which we interpret the events. The storm of body dissatisfaction blew with hurricane force in my life when the unexpected happened to my body after pregnancy.

I have a small frame with a short torso. When I became pregnant with my oldest daughter, I carried her all out front. I became so large my maternity clothes didn't fit around the middle for the last month. There was only one tent type dress I could wear with any comfort. That was a new experience for my 110 pound, 5'4" frame. After she was born, the stretch marks on my stomach were terrible. The skin hung down and I no longer had a belly button. It was a strange oval indentation with skin hanging around it. I was repulsed. I eagerly asked the doctor at my post-partum check-up when my middle would return to normal. He looked at me smiling and said that "skin isn't very forgiving." When you carry the way I did, the stretching usually doesn't go back to normal. I went home and cried for days. I was devastated when it didn't happen according to my plan. My stomach was the body part I loved! Now it was this ugly mass of purple, wrinkled hanging skin with no recognizable belly button.

I am a little embarrassed to say that at first, I was very upset with God. I was trying to obey the plan God showed me for a family. Why did this have to happen to me? I started making comparisons with growing envy—many women tinier than me sailed through pregnancy and didn't have a problem. Proverbs 20:27 says, "The spirit of a man is the lamp of the Lord, Searching all the inner depths of his heart." As soon as God wasn't fulfilling His plan for my life the way I expected, the pride and covetousness that were hiding in the depths of my heart came up in full force. Looking back, the last thing I really needed was to immediately go back to my original figure, so I could walk around smug and self-satisfied about how well I handled pregnancy. I would have annoyed everyone with my exercise tips.

Today I realize God loved me too much to just let me walk in pride. He saw what I could not back then. He decided I needed the humility and strength that is part of godly character much more than a perfectly chiseled abdomen. The Holy Spirit convicted me with the question I always have to answer whenever I am disappointed with the results of following God's plan: Do I trust God and believe that whatever happens will eventually work for my good even if I don't feel it or understand it at the time? It always comes back to that question, doesn't it? Do we trust Him?

Paul says, "For to be carnally minded is enmity against God; for it is not subject to the law of God, nor can be. So then, those who are in the flesh cannot please God" (Romans 8:7-8). You have to trust God, through faith (which does please Him) beyond what you can see for now—especially in your disappointments and insecurities. Once that becomes your heart attitude, God usually makes a way to bless you in the very things you completely hand over to him. Then it is a blessing rather than a distraction or pride trip "and He adds no sorrow to it" (Proverbs 10:22).

God kept working on my pride, and I actually did get a mommy makeover 12 years after my last child. Yay—I had a round belly button again! I also now have great compassion for others struggling with body issues, which would not be the case if circumstances I could not control had not happened to me. It was a blessing, and I see it now. God was working on something much more important in my life, and I would not want it any other way.

I want to challenge you to organize your day according to strengthening your spirit through prayer and reading the Word. In God's beauty plan, building the spirit and caring for your inner person is what will make you radiant and build confidence on a much deeper level. The outer man comes second. Make praying and reading the Word the main goal on your to-do list each and every day. The time it takes to read one chapter of the Bible is 3-5 minutes. Bible tapes are very handy as you drive to and from work. I know several women who travel as a part of their jobs and throughout their day, and they use car and plane time to do their reading and praying regularly. I know that in certain seasons such as when you have a baby, studying in depth might be a challenge, but getting the word in you brings benefits, even if you cannot sit down for an hour to study. That 5 minutes will not return empty (Isaiah 55:11).

Prayer can be done all day, even in split second "love-connections," uniting your heart to Him whether you are thanking Him, leaning on Him, asking Him to meet a need, or telling God you love Him and appreciate Him. I don't recommend you live on split second connections as your main communication with God, but they are wonderful booster shots to your spirit through the day. I have learned to invite the Holy Spirit in all day to guide and lead me as I work or talk to people. It amazes me the way things come to my mind that people later tell me really made a difference in their lives. I also realize things practically and see things that I did not before. God actively works in and through me each day because I turn my attention to Him.

It never gets old! One time, I was in a session with a couple who were particularly argumentative and negative with each other. As the session continued, I began to be discouraged, I invited the Holy Spirit to give me the wisdom I desperately needed to try to reset the session more productively. I told them we can use our words negatively and build negative patterns, then proceeded to give examples of what that looks like in communication. As I gave the examples, both of their eyes got wide. The husband said it seemed as if I secretly taped their conversations. They became very quiet and really attentive to what they could do to change. The Holy Spirit specifically gave me a word of knowledge, bringing those examples to my mind. It always blesses each time that happens, which illustrates the goodness of God as we invite Him to partner with us.

God will continue to help you every time you fail to be consistent. He is delighted you desire to spend time with Him, and that you keep trying. Psalm 37:23-24 promises that even if you fall God will uphold you so you will not be utterly cast down. Eventually, you will succeed, get through the barriers, and never want to go back to not spending quality time with God in prayer and His word again, no matter what. That might mean a little less sleep, skipping the show, skipping the gym (once in a while), keeping your Bible open on the kitchen counter while you cook, listening to Bible while showering, or driving. Whatever it takes. It is too valuable to not do. The resolve to get there has to remain, or the habit will not stick. Isaiah 50:7 says, "For the Lord God will help me; therefore, I will not be disgraced; Therefore, I have set my face like a flint, and I know that I will not be ashamed." This references the determination Jesus had to accomplish His goal. If you set your face like flint and determine that you will not give up, you will get there, and the results will be amazing. Your diamond beauty will be developing on the inside as your foundation.

Strengthen your spirit first.

CHAPTER TWO

Soul Strength

The soul encompasses our will, thoughts, intellect, and emotions. Let's clarify what soul strength looks like from God's perspective and how it is part of God's plan to make you beautiful.

The number of women who secretly (or openly) struggle with anxiety, depression, and lack of confidence always amazes me as I work in my field as a therapist. According to US government data, approximately 12 million women will experience clinical depression in a single year and 1in 8 can plan to experience clinical depression in their lifetime.[10]

As a therapist, I have encouraging news to those of you who battle with these issues: you *will* begin to think more clearly and become stable emotionally as you continue the fight. In my thirty-two years of professional and pastoral counseling, I have seen women conquer depression and anxiety as they continued to pray, seek help professionally and spiritually, and trust God.

"God has not given us a *spirit* of fear, but of power and of love and of a *sound mind.*" (2 Tim 1:7). The word *sound mind* here in Greek is *sophronismos* (Strong's #4995). It is a combination of *sos,* meaning safe, and *phren*, meaning the mind; hence, *safe-thinking*. Safe thinking means having good judgment, disciplined thought patterns, and the ability to understand and make right decisions. It also includes the qualities of self-control and self-discipline.[11] Let that soak in for a minute. God has a powerful plan for your soul. The apostle Paul is stating we have a will (mind, thoughts, intellect) and heart (feelings), which is what our soul consists of, that will be able to work optimally, so we will be women who make right decisions and have appropriate emotional reactions in everyday life. He says we will be able to live a self-controlled life. Imagine the savings in therapy visits alone. All that will be possible because God has given us *the spirit* (pnuema or breath, [*Strong's* #4151]) of power, love and "safe thinking." The pnuema Paul is referring to is the Spirit we discussed in the last section. Are you beginning to see how essential it is to build from the inside-out? Fullness of His Spirit operating in us makes "optimal soul operation" possible. One builds on the other.

When it comes to our soul, God made us to function from the inside-out psychologically, too. Our thoughts affect our feelings, which affect our actions—that's the classic cognitive-behavioral triangle many therapists use in CBT therapy as a basic premise. Our thinking is key to how we feel and act. Numbers 13:33 illustrates this point by explaining how the Israelites saw themselves as grasshoppers in their own sight and "so they were." It stopped them from taking the land God promised to give them, even though God was on their side and they were well able to do it. As a result, they were stuck in misery for forty years. That is why we absolutely have to stay in God's Word to focus on who we are created to be and how God sees us. Otherwise, we get trapped in how we see ourselves, which is never as complete, capable, and full of potential as God sees us.

We attain a strong mind through the developing good judgment, understanding, and disciplined thought patterns. Let's explore in detail how to do this.

Developing Good Judgment and Understanding

Good judgment is the ability to make a decision, or form an objective opinion, authoritatively, and wisely. It means to have good sense. Understanding includes discernment and enlightened intelligence.[12] Does that sound a little lofty or intimidating? Paul advises to "hold fast to the pattern of *sound words* which you have *heard* from me." These sound words are the teachings of scripture which Paul goes on to say in 1 Timothy 3:16 are profitable for "instruction in righteousness," or in other words, training in right living. The Word of God plays a crucial role in helping us develop wisdom and discernment which are foundational to true good judgment and understanding. Keywords here are "hearing" and "speaking". Jerry Bridges says in *The Practice of Godliness*,

"The most common method of scriptural intake is *hearing* the Word of God taught to us by our pastors and teachers. We are living in a day when this method tends to be lightly regarded by many people as a somewhat ineffective means of learning spiritual truth. This is serious error…One reason the hearing of the Word of God has fallen into such low esteem is that we do not obey God's teaching in Revelation 1:3: 'Blessed are those who hear it and take heart what is written in it.' Too often today we listen to be entertained instead of instructed, to be moved emotionally rather than moved to obedience. We do not take to heart what we hear and apply it to our lives."[13]

We must hear the Word regularly and "hold it fast" or apply it and continue to live in it (1 Tim. 3:14). The result of this will be as Paul says in verse 15, "to make you wise for salvation through faith which is in Christ Jesus" for the purpose that "the man of God may be complete, thoroughly equipped for every good work (I Timothy 3:17).

The pattern we see here to develop optimal judgment and understanding is to hear, apply, and continue in God's word. All three have to be active in our lives, otherwise, we will not grow and change. Our minds need to be instructed with truth so we can walk wisely in every practical area of our lives. When something is absolutely true, you can trust it and apply it with confidence in your life.

After we hear God's word, we need to apply it by "speaking" it to ourselves and others. Speaking things is a powerful principle that makes them real. There's a creative power in speaking that I am not going to go into more detail with right now, but if you know anyone familiar with quantum physics, they can explain sound wave particles to you. Just as God spoke the universe into existence, you, being made in His image, can speak things into motion and change the atmosphere both positively and negatively. Proverbs 18:21says, "Death and life are in the power of the tongue, And those who love it will eat its fruit." I did that with my math ability. I was an honors math student until I hit my sophomore year in high school. I had a hard time in class and kept telling myself, out of my discouragement, that I could not learn the material anymore. I did poorly in math for the next 2 years and avoided the subject for most of my life.

Declaring God's promises and meditating on his word constantly, makes us like "a tree planted by rivers of water, that brings forth its fruit in its season, whose leaf also shall not wither, and whatever he does shall prosper," (Psalm 1:3) What we think about will affect how we feel which determines our decisions to act.

Developing Disciplined Thought Patterns

There are two parts to developing disciplined thought patterns. The first is to pull down (demolish) any thoughts that are not in accordance with the true knowledge of God, "bringing every thought into captivity to the obedience of Christ" as it says in 2 Corinthians 10:5. The word "obedience" (Strong's #5218) here is made up of two Greek words *hupo* (or under), and *akouo* (to hear). Again, in order to develop safe-thinking, active hearing is critical. We have to *listen with the intent to actively reject whatever we believe about ourselves that does not line up with the Truth of what God says about us.*

Every stronghold (a thought that has rooted in your mind and goes against the Truth of what God says) is a lie because it goes against God's ways of thinking about us. False philosophies and beliefs about who we are lead us to live in fear because we accept lies about what makes us valuable and worthy of love. Paul tells us we have to demolish these lies not by our own efforts ("according to the flesh" in 2 Corinthians 10:3), but according to God's power (2 Corinthians 10:4, 1Timothy 1:7) by His presence with us *through the Holy Spirit* which Jesus sent to "guide us into all truth" (John 16:7-14). The Holy Spirit is the lamp that reveals what you need to demolish in your life.

After watching one of my daughters change into a fearful, angry person, I had a front row seat to how a stronghold of lies takes hold of a person's thoughts and distorts them. My daughter's personality, self-perception, and confidence totally changed as her anorexia grew. The more she focused on the food and diet concerns, the more she "fed" those concerns and strengthened them. They became her idol. What, in the beginning, was something that brought satisfaction became her source of pain and grief. Then fear came in and controlled her thoughts. The questions of what would happen if she let go of the anorexia plagued her. The fear of being fat and out of control became her harsh taskmaster until her

5'7" frame was only 97 lbs. The whole day was focused on guarding her eating disorder and figuring out how she could maintain it.

Jim, my husband, and I had noticed for a few months that she was getting thinner, but were unaware of the hold anorexia already had on her mind and heart. Anytime her father and I tried to say something, she became so defensive and angry, we would retreat. I knew I had to confront her and not back down. Finally, it was a 3 day weekend and she had eaten barely anything. She looked so unhappy. I realized this wasn't just a phase that would work itself out on its own as I had been initially hoping.

The very night I was prayerfully planning to talk to her, my daughter realized she could no longer pretend everything was fine. She came to me in tears saying she was worried about her health because she was getting dizzy during random times of the day, every day. As I held her hand quietly not sure what to say, she began to cry harder and harder. All the agony of the past few months, the lies about eating with friends or at track meets, the fear of gaining any weight came tumbling out. I made an appointment with her pediatrician and we considered what to do. Within days of our talk, the teenage daughter of a business associate of my husband's died suddenly of heart failure from the devastating effects of her eating disorder. The timing drove home to all of us, especially our daughter, the reality of what allowing this stronghold to grow would eventually mean. We immediately took action to help her.

After she recovered, my daughter told me, she literally had a voice in her head directing her actions. When she went to the pantry or refrigerator it would say, "Don't eat anything. You won't be able to stop if you do." When she would walk away, the voice would say, "Good job. If you did it this time you can do it again."

Eventually, she realized she had to *actively* reject that voice if she was going to destroy the hold anorexia had on her mind. The thoughts had to be pulled down. How? Ephesians 6:16-17 explains the word of God is the sword of the Spirit that will dismantle those wrong thoughts. The shield of faith—which comes by *hearing* and meditating on the word of God as we spoke of before—has to be held up to deflect the evil darts, the lies, the enemy throws at you to try to destroy you. Then the sword has to be used for the combat process to counteract the lies we are hearing in our mind. The type of sword referenced in Ephesians 6 is actually a small dagger for hand-to-hand combat. The soldiers would also use it to dig out any darts that got past their shields, minimizing any damage the enemy tried to inflict so the healing could start immediately.

The second part of disciplined thought is to actively replace the old thoughts with those that are life-giving and positive. We have to take out the word of God and use it to counteract any lies attacking our minds by applying it for correction until God's word becomes our reality. Do not underestimate the power of this because it sounds simple. As a therapist, I have watched people's lives be greatly affected by the things they chose to dwell on and think about each day. Jesus explained that when a person is delivered from oppression and an old way of thinking, if his heart stays empty, evil comes back and tries to take over again (Matthew 12:43-45). You become open to even greater deception. You need to fill the empty space with God's Word. Paul encourages the Philippians,

"Finally, brethren, whatever things are true, whatever things are noble, whatever things are just, whatever things are pure, whatever things are lovely, whatever things are of good report, if there is any virtue and if there is anything praiseworthy—meditate on these things. The things which you l*earned and received and* *heard and saw* in me, these do, *and the God of peace will be with you.*" (Philippians 4:8-9 NKJV).

Isaiah 26:3-4 says, "You will keep him in perfect peace, whose mind is stayed on You, because he trusts in You. Trust in the Lord forever, for in YAH, the Lord, is *everlasting strength.*"

The negative thoughts, which twist our ability to develop diamond beauty, tear us down emotionally. When we are torn down emotionally, we are affected physically. When you pull down the strongholds and replace them with meditating on the good things Paul lists above, you will have the peace to make good decisions.

Body Strength

God is also interested in your body reflecting His glory. He always works on the whole package. In Philippians 1:6, Paul writes,

"Being confident of this very thing, that He who has begun a *good* work in you will complete it until the day of Jesus Christ..."

The word "good" (Strong's #18) is *agathos* in the Greek which literally means good in an aesthetic and moral sense suggesting attractiveness *physically* and morally.

As I said in the last section, your thoughts, if focused on negativity, can cause anxiety and fear. These have profound effects on your body "drying up your bones", and robbing you of peace (Proverbs 16:23, 24; 17:22) That is why it is important to meditate on good things. Jesus said that what is in your heart will come out of your mouth (Luke 6:45). "Good reports" (as Paul calls them in Philippians 4:8, referring to gracious, kind words) actually keep the bones healthy (Proverbs 15:30).

Peace is a huge component to being able to have a healthy body. Fear and anxiety literally produce a stress hormone in your brain called cortisol. This is one thing I have observed regularly in my work with people who live in high stress or trauma affected situations. When the body is producing excessive stress hormones continually, it can have many adverse effects. In essence, it breaks the body down over time. High levels of cortisol will cause:

- healthy bone and muscles to become weak and fragile
- deceleration in cell regeneration
- a decrease in the body's ability to heal itself and ward off illness

- a hindrance in digestion and metabolism, causing stomach disorders and weight gain especially around the midsection.[14]
- short term memory impairment, making it very difficult for someone to learn or retain information.

Sleep is an important way God blesses us through peace. Psalm 127:2 says, "It is vain for you to rise up early, To sit up late, To eat the bread of sorrows; For so He gives His beloved sleep." Sleep in that passage literally refers to deep peace. This is a foundational beauty and health contributor. It reduces stress, helps our skin and body to rejuvenate, lowers our anxiety, and helps us to eat better. Sleep and metabolism are closely linked. If you don't sleep enough, you have a tendency to make poor food choices, and you will usually overeat.[15]

God intends for you to turn to Him like a child and to have rest for your soul and in turn your body (Psalm 131). Psalm 34:4,5 says, "I *sought the Lord* and he heard me, and delivered me out of all my fears. They looked to Him and were radiant and their faces were not ashamed."

Diamond beauty begins by following God's Inside-out Plan in our spirit, then soul, and finally having the outcome be visible in our bodies. One builds and enhances the other resulting in radiance.

Note: If You Are Struggling with an Eating Disorder

If you are trapped in an eating disorder or headed that way, or if you have a loved one that has one, there is hope. God will help you un-pry the grip this stronghold has on your mind.

First, ask the Holy Spirit to show you the ways your thinking is twisted. If you are sincere, He will begin to open your eyes. You will need help from others. The Bible says there is safety in a multitude of counselors (Prov.24:6).

Proverbs 18:1 says, "A man who isolates himself seeks his own desire; He rages against all wise judgment." A strategy of the enemy is to isolate you so that you are much more vulnerable and without anyone who can speak truth to you. Women no longer want to be in close relationships with friends or family because they do not want to be told the truth about how they look or act. My beautiful, social daughter spent more and more time alone or exercising. She plotted how she could avoid meals with us. The eating disorder will tell you, "you are alone and no one understands you." It becomes your constant companion, always present in the back of your mind. Ask yourself: Do I believe God loves me? Do my family/friends love me? Would they really be worried and tell me I have a problem if I didn't? Why won't I trust them or listen to what they have to say? If eating and living this way is so good for me, why am I so miserable and afraid to let go? You have to be willing to face the honest answers to those questions and take action to pull down the lies. Trust God, your parents, friends, husband, boyfriend or kids. They love you and want to help. Go to someone who has walked through it for an honest talk and seek a competent counselor. God will help you and life will be good again.

Note: To Parents

If you are a parent of a child struggling with this issue, take charge of the authority you have been given by God over your child and take the responsibility of eating out of your child's hands until his or her perspective is clear and he or she is free. People get better in hospitals because they no longer have the option of not eating. They are monitored and forced to eat until they are stronger. The problem is that after release, the strongholds are still intact, and the cycle starts all over. Be brave and tell her she no longer has to deal with this on her own and she can fully blame you for fighting the eating disorder for her. Tell her as a united family that you love her too much to let the eating disorder have her. Then be determined that as she rages and refuses to let go, you will be praying and setting your face like stone until each food battle is won. Although you might not be able to win every one, little by little you will take back ground. God will help you. Turn to Him before each meal asking for wisdom and grace. Cast your cares on Him for He cares for you (Psalm 55:22; I Peter 5:7).

Many parents are hesitant to do this, but trust me that it is the key. Coming alongside her and being her strength until she can do it on her own again takes a lot of pressure off of her. My husband and I had to do this for my daughter and we are so glad we did. Our daughter told us that even though she fought us, she was very relieved when it was no longer in her control and she didn't have to carry it alone. She wouldn't admit it then, but she wanted us to help her deep down.

As a therapist, I strongly urge you to go to competent health professionals for advice on how to help most effectively. As a parent, and as Christians, God made us to be part of a body and not to stand alone. We have to be one another's hands and feet when necessary. The outcomes for people who have family support and treatment are much better than if this is just dealt with individually. If you are interested in more information and help, I recommend La Grange and Lock's book, *Help Your Teenager Beat an Eating Disorder.* I have used it as a mom and therapist. It is tremendously helpful.

Chapter 3
Salvation: God's Beauty Process

The Inside-Out beauty plan becomes a reality through the continual process of restoration called salvation. Salvation is a common word in the Christian community, but many people simply define it as the initial moment you surrender your life to Jesus and are going to heaven. This is true, but it is only the beginning. The Greek word *soteria* (Strong's #4991) says "salvation" is deliverance, preservation, soundness, prosperity, happiness, and general well-being. Salvation is the all-encompassing work God has done in His death and resurrection to restore us in every way from the fallen state we are born into. To restore means "to make something acceptable or pleasant in spite of its negative qualities or aspects."[16]

Psalm 149:4 tells us "the Lord takes pleasure in His people; He will beautify the humble with salvation." He takes pleasure in you. You make Him happy, so He wants to beautify you. It is not an option for God to beautify you—as though He picks and chooses those whom He will beautify. God beautifies *every* believer who humbly walks with God.

Psalm 103:1-5 lays out the 5 parts of restoration God applies to you through your life. Positionally, you are saved in a moment, but it takes your whole life to come into the completeness of that. God always has more than we expect or think (Ephesians 3:20).

Are you ready? In this chapter, we will take an in-depth look at these benefits and how to walk in them so you transform into a woman of diamond beauty "whose worth is far above rubies" (Proverbs 31:10.)

We begin with David commanding his soul (thoughts, intellect and emotions) to line up with God's benefits and to remember to praise God for these good things. He writes: "Bless the Lord, O my soul; And all that is within me, bless His holy name! Bless the Lord, O my soul, And forget not all His benefits: Who forgives all your iniquities, Who heals all your diseases, Who redeems your life from destruction, Who crowns you with lovingkindness and tender mercies, Who satisfies your mouth with good things, So that your youth is renewed like the eagle's." (Psalm 103:1-5)

Of the 5 parts of the Benefit Package we receive when we give our lives to the Lord, the first three are what God spares us from and the last two are what He specifically blesses us with, as His daughters. This package as a whole makes us truly beautiful from the inside-out as we keep applying the benefits fully to our lives.

1) God "forgives all your iniquities." (Psalm 103:3)

The beginning of the salvation restoration process is being forgiven of all of our sins (1 John 1:9, 4:10). Forgiveness to us and from us is critical to understand so we can reflect God's glory. When forgiven, we are rescued from the guilt, shame and weight of how we have fallen short—all of it. That little word "all" is important here because the enemy tries to stop us from total freedom by whispering doubt into our minds that we cannot be totally for. *All* of your sins are forgiven. It's *done*. Jesus paid for everything on the cross.

Forgiveness of sins frees a man, erasing all his "debt," and clearing his conscience. "As far as the east is from the west, so far has He removed our transgressions from us" says Psalm 103:12. Getting the weight of our past lifted and being free has the power to change the countenance and emotional make-up of a person in a single moment, as it did for my college friend, Dawn.

I transferred to a real party school in upstate New York, after my initial start at the Fashion Institute of Technology (FIT). Partying several nights a week was normal. I loved it—at first. After a few months, I realized I couldn't live this way. It was starting to really affect my sleep, and the superficial romantic relationships with men left me feeling unvalued and guarded. I also found myself wanting to drink every day to deal with the stress of life and school. As the downward spiral continued, one Sunday, during my second semester, I felt particularly discouraged as another weekend was winding down. I went to the student union to get a salad to try to buffer the toll the weekend flurry of partying had taken on my body, and this girl I knew from high school walked in. She smiled widely and was literally glowing. It was such a contrast to the hung-over, bleary-eyed people all around her. I shouted out to her, "Hey Dawn!" She turned around and the excitement of recognition and surprise took over. "Oh my gosh, Dona! I didn't know you went to school here!" I smiled back, "I didn't know you were here either. I usually see people from our high school when I go downtown, but I never see you."

Downtown was the epicenter of the bars and parties. Her response floored me, "I usually don't go downtown. I am a Christian. In fact, I am just coming back from church." So that explained it. She was glowing because of the freedom and joy she experienced after being in the presence of God and fellowship, rather than the effects of sin I grappled with more and more. Through her kindness and genuine care, she became the connection that led me to recommit my heart to the Lord a few days later. Soon I was the one walking into my dorm smiling and full of life on Sundays as my peers tried to get over their hang-overs. Then many of them started coming to me wondering what changed in me that was now making me glow.

Forgiveness is not just a one-time occurrence. It is a daily, continual process of restoration to make us a beautiful reflection of God's glory. It's a lifestyle. When a person falls, (which she will do because as Paul says in Romans 7:15 "For what I am doing, I do not understand. For what I will to do, that I do not practice; but what I hate, that I do") she runs to her God. She repents, and is immediately forgiven because of the blood of Jesus.

"There is now therefore no condemnation" says Romans 8:1. It is a continual exchange of self for Christ in us—His blood, His power, His strength in exchange for our sin, and our weakness. I can attest that it is a life-giving, continual exchange I have experienced for almost 40 years now since that fateful day at the student union.

Where does the continuing diamond beauty development come in? The next step is to allow the glory of what God has done for us to extend to others, which allows us to imitate God as his dear children by turning to our fellow man and forgiving them. First, we get free and then we walk in freedom and dispense grace to others through a life of practicing forgiveness. We shine when we do not carry around anger, pain, and shame of offenses, whether they are ones we have committed or ones that have been done against us.

Jesus said hurts and offenses against us "must come" while we are on this earth (Matt 18:7; Luke 17:1). They are a certainty. Diamond beauty gets developed when the pressure of pain and hurt is met with obedience to God's principles so we can stand against it and overcome it (Luke 6:46-49). That's how we become unconquerable which is the definition of diamond in Greek.

What does walking in forgiveness really look like? In Matthew 18:21-35 Jesus gives us a blueprint for how God expects us to handle our hurts, which He frequently refers to as the debts people owe us. In the Matthew 18 parable, the king deciding to "settle accounts" with one who owed him a great debt, models two key aspects of walking in biblical forgiveness: first, forgiveness, and second, it requires mercy and compassion.

You may have tried the forgiveness process many times. It might be difficult for you and seem like it doesn't work. Don't believe that you haven't forgiven someone just because the hurts require a period of time to heal. If you have a deep cut on your arm, you can treat it immediately, but it doesn't feel healed immediately. I would advise you to keep working on it. The process involves prayerfully laying down each wave of hurt or anger as it comes at the feet of God, asking the Holy Spirit (the Comforter) to heal you, and then releasing the pain and exchanging it for His grace.

Note: The Steps of the Forgiveness Process

1. Acknowledge your emotions and how you have been hurt. Acknowledge the pain, the feelings you have

about it and why it has hurt you so much. Identifying the feelings helps clarify the effect they have on you emotionally and physically. This is like cleaning out the "infection" of the hurt in your heart. It is painful, but an important part of the process if you want to really heal. Many people find it helpful to write this out or to speak to someone about it. Confession, or verbalizing things in our heart out loud, is an important part of healing. It allows others to support us and/or pray for us while we complete the process.

2. Write down and recognize the specific hurts, so you can really face what others have done and what you feel owed. Don't minimize any of the hurts or the feelings; be totally honest to yourself about the extent of the hurt, otherwise you won't be cleaning out all the "infection."

3. Realize and come to terms with the fact that the person who hurt you will not be able to pay you back what they owe. In many cases, that is just not possible. If your father abused you for years, he can never pay back what he took from you. There is grief associated with loss, and to really forgive we have to face our grief and anger and walk through it honestly. Unresolved grief or anger can keep us stuck in unforgiveness.

4. Choose to have compassion on the debtor. A synonym for compassion is mercy. You need to exchange the anger you have for them with choosing to have mercy on them for what they did. Mercy can be a choice without being a feeling. Again take it to the altar. Whatever you lay down, God fills up with love.

5. Speak the words of forgiveness out loud to the person who hurt you, whether in person or to God, stating the specific thing you are forgiving them for as you allow your heart to recognize the pain. It is important to use wisdom and possibly the counsel of others if you aren't sure if you should physically face the person. The purpose is release and freedom for you as much as for them. Many times, people who have hurt us may not be aware (or be able to accept) the extent of the pain hey caused. After the confession, rip up the account, whether the literal paper or the account you have carried in your heart. Completely release them.

6. Begin to pray for them to be blessed, especially in the area they hurt you. If possible, ask God to show you how you can bless them in any way He desires—by continuing to pray for them, helping them in any way they might need it, and/or showing kindness to them when/if you see them.

7. The devil will try to tempt you to go back to unforgiveness so he can make sure you are wasting precious time and energy being miserable and angry. He will tell you that because you are tempted, you never really forgave in the first place. If the temptation to hold them accountable again comes back into your mind, immediately release it to God declaring that you meant your forgiveness. Turn your thoughts to pray blessing for them. Remember that intentional acts of your will do not require your emotions to be in line with them. Eventually, the anger and grief will melt away as you keep walking through the process.

Over the years, I have seen God do miraculous restorations in relationships and lives as forgiveness flowed between couples and families. I remember one young client I had who came in devastated when she found that her husband had become addicted to pornography. She was so hurt and broken, desperate to find healing and an answer as to why he would do this. They had only been married a few years, so she felt she must have a deficit in herself if he turned to porn because he must not be satisfied. She was also very angry at the betrayal. Her heart was broken, causing weight loss, due to stress, and difficulty sleeping. She wasn't sure she could ever forgive him or trust him again. Fear that forgiveness won't be possible, or the outright refusal to forgive, is a common reaction when hurt is deep.

Although we need some time to process the hurt initially, when people have difficulty forgiving, sometimes they have a misunderstanding of how forgiveness restores life and growth to their own hearts. Forgiveness is freedom. An unpaid debt binds both people who have to carry it. The one who is owed has to carry around a record of it for as long as she tries to collect. That is a burden that takes up a lot of space in our minds and hearts, keeping us tied to the painful past like an invisible rope. We aren't free to move forward in an emotionally healthy way, in human relationships or in our relationship with God, with that rope tied around us. We block the flow of forgiveness as Jesus explained when He prayed "and forgive us our debts, as we forgive our debtors" in Matthew 6:12 and 18:34, 35.

Another block is when people think forgiveness cheapens their pain because it lets the other person off the hook without proper restitution. When you look at the king in the parable we discussed above in Matthew 18, he didn't minimize what the servant owed him. He realized the servant could never pay back what he had taken. Then the king's heart got involved. Matt 18:27 says "Then the master of that servant was moved with compassion, released him and forgave him the debt." The word "moved" literally means deep pity from the seat of His emotions. In His heart, the king chose to let the debt go and extended mercy. Don't you hope others will forgive you for the ways you have hurt them? I have never heard anyone say they hope someone will hate them forever because they offended them. They might know they don't deserve to be forgiven, but deep down everyone hopes it is possible. What a blessing it is for us to have the capacity to be merciful.

    Back to my client who first had to work through the grief she experienced because of how her relationship with her husband forever changed because of porn. As she eventually worked the steps of forgiveness when she was ready and continued until the wound healed, she discovered that not only did she have a deeper understanding of grace (she was very judgmental before) but her husband and she became closer than ever as they navigated how to really build emotional and physical intimacy. God used that betrayal to heal so much in her. She literally developed a graciousness about her that was truly beautiful to be around.

On the flip side, unacknowledged sin and refusing to forgive others is very detrimental to our mental and physical health. That is the final benefit forgiveness of sin has for us as we pursue diamond beauty. In Psalm 32 David wrote:

"Blessed is he whose transgression is forgiven, Whose sin is covered. Blessed is the man to whom the Lord does not impute iniquity, And in whose spirit there is no deceit. When I kept silent, my bones grew old, Through my groaning all the day long… My vitality was turned into the drought of summer."

Unforgiveness ages us and makes us more susceptible to disease. Our immune system weakens when we are emotionally stressed and feeling bad about ourselves/the people who hurt us. When we carry our offense and refuse to forgive others we "groan all the day long" as our thoughts torture us (Matt 18:34). We feel depressed and exhausted: "our bones grow old" and our "vitality" is dried up. (Psalm 32:3-4). Have you ever noticed the hard, grim appearance of a person who is twisted up by bitterness? Forgiveness keeps our heart pliable and our countenance soft because we are extending mercy and grace.

2) God "heals all your diseases." (Psalm 103:3 NKJ)

This is a huge topic that has filled pages of many books. The aspect of healing we will focus on is simply the fact that healing and health are a part of the restoration process God empowers us to live in when we get saved. Healing certainly makes us reflect His glory and beauty.

In Psalm 103:3, we see the word "all" meaning that every disease is under the Benefit Package of salvation. Days after God brought the Israelites out of Egypt, He promised, "If you listen carefully to the Lord your God and do what is right in his eyes, if you pay attention to his commands and keep all his decrees, I will not bring on you any of the diseases I brought on the Egyptians, for I am the Lord, who heals you." (Exodus 15:26). God established healing as a provision right from the beginning of the relationship with his own people that would set them apart from the world.

Healing and faith are linked throughout both the Old and New Testaments. From the verse above, to the statements Jesus made it is clear that faith affects healing. There is only one definition in the Bible of faith, and it is found in Hebrews 11:1. The Amplified version offers a beautiful translation for deeper understanding: "Now faith is the assurance (title deed, confirmation) of things hoped for (divinely guaranteed), and the evidence of things not seen [the conviction of their reality—faith comprehends as fact what cannot be experienced by the physical senses]." When we choose to think and act according to what we are "divinely guaranteed" rather than the earthly circumstance we see, the circumstances begin to line up with our faith. It is the way the Inside-Out plan works. The spirit affects the soul which affects the body.

Reading that Hebrews 11:1 definition in the Amplified version helps to clarify why Jesus frequently said a person's faith made them well. It was a fact for them. Even the faith of a friend, parent, or boss would lead to a person getting healed (Matthew 8 and 9; Luke 7:1-10; Mark 7:25-30). You can walk in faith for others and see their lives changed. It is a similar principle to forgiveness.

This happened to my mom when she was healed of her brain tumor. My dad became a Christian when I was 14 years old. He changed from a serious drinker, cheater, and physically abusive husband and father to a faith-filled man who would sit and read the Bible for hours. I didn't know what to make of it, but I was thrilled to no longer be afraid of what the day would bring once the

Vodka bottle came out of the cupboard. My mom liked it, but also didn't trust it at the same time. She made it clear she didn't want any part of this new "religious weirdness." A few months after his salvation, my mom was diagnosed with a brain tumor. She had been having headaches for several months, but refused to go to the doctor because her mom died of a brain tumor. It scared her into denial. When she blacked out while they were leaving the supermarket one day, my dad insisted she get examined by a doctor.

Her worst fears were confirmed. A tumor the size of an egg was growing, and they weren't sure it was operable. At that time, my mom was attending a Catholic church. My dad was told a large Catholic charismatic conference was going to be held a few hours away and that healing was going to be one of the topics at the workshops. My dad, as he prayed for her, was convinced she should go and that the Lord would heal her. He would not take "no" for an answer. Feeling so sick and wondering if my dad was crazy, she very reluctantly, out of desperation, agreed. While sitting in the back of one of the workshops, she was wonderfully healed. Even though my mom wasn't walking with God until after her healing, my dad's prayer and faith resulted in healing for her. My mom's tumor became one of her favorite testimonies of God's goodness. She had great faith afterwards for healing and would regularly pray for others to be healed.

Healing can be a touchy subject, though. Full provision has been made by Jesus through the cross to heal all diseases (Matthew 8:17; John 10:10; James 5:14-16; 1 Peter 2:24), but everyone doesn't get healed.

Why does this happen? I regularly hear comments from people questioning if they are somehow being punished or overlooked by God when they or a loved one is walking through sickness. The disciples wondered that also when they asked Jesus why a man was born blind, assuming he or his parents had sinned, Jesus told them very clearly "Neither this man nor his parents sinned, but that the works of God should be revealed in him." (John 9:1-3NKJ). Sometimes, as human beings living in a fallen world, we live between the provisions which are part of our "inheritance" as God's children (Eph. 1:18) and the circumstances we walk in with sickness. We are called to believe and praise God, even though His ways are beyond what we understand. (Psalm 145:3)

There are only a few examples in the Old and New Testament that give us a picture of the persistence and warfare needed to overcome. One is when Jesus came down from the transfiguration and there was an uproar over a little boy who was not able to be healed/delivered by His disciples: "Then the disciples came to Jesus privately and said, "Why could we not cast it out?" So Jesus said to them, "Because of your unbelief; for assuredly, I say to you, if you have faith as a mustard seed, you will say to this mountain, 'Move from here to there,' and it will move; and nothing will be impossible for you. However, this kind does not go out except by prayer and fasting." (Matthew 17:19-21 NKJV) Sometimes, we have to persistently pray and fast for healing or deliverance.

How many of us assume, or have rationalized, that it must be God's plan or a person's fault that there is illness? That is actually contrary to what the Word clearly teaches, which makes it a false belief. But for a season God allows us to persist in prayer and turn our hearts more deeply to Him before we see healing or go home to heaven. 1 Peter 4:1-2 states, "Therefore, since Christ suffered for us in the flesh, arm yourselves also with the same mind, for he who has suffered in the flesh has ceased from sin, that he no longer should live the rest of his time in the flesh for the lusts of men, but for the will of God."

This is not done simply for the sake of cruel suffering. God loves you so much, He wants what will benefit you most in the end. There are many testimonies of saints who didn't give up, but trusted the Lord through physical trials and were eventually restored.

Job is the classic example of a man God allowed to go through disease for a season. His declaration of His faith in God despite his disease and loss in Job 13:15 stands as our standard through the ages: "Though He slay me, yet will I trust Him. Even so, I will defend my own ways before Him." Job couldn't understand the "why" of what was happening, but he developed humility and received even greater blessing in the end as he continued to trust God and hold on to his integrity. God never explains to Job the reason He allowed Satan to afflict his body, but interestingly, God instructed him to pray for His friends so God would accept them. Here is another example of forgiveness and healing being linked. As he obediently prayed for these men who were condemning and accusatory, telling Job he was sick because of some moral defect, God restored every loss Job experienced and he lived to the age of 140 (Job 42:10-17).

God will beautify you with His salvation as you walk in humility and faith, trusting and standing on healing as one of His benefits.

3) God "redeems your life from destruction." (Psalm 103:4 NKJ)

The next benefit David lists is redemption from destruction. In Psalm 103:4, David says that God buys us back and rescues us from hell, or "the pit," as our kinsman redeemer. In biblical times, a kinsman redeemer was the nearest relative to someone who would pay for their debt or help them in any way they needed to get out of trouble. They took full responsibility for them. Kinsman redeemer is the same word used in Ezekiel 16:8 when God expresses to Israel, His bride, how she became His and entered into a covenant with Him, belonging to Him. "I swore an oath to you and entered into a covenant with you, and you became Mine," says the Lord God."

There are two important points here to stop and look at in order to successfully walk in restoration so we can shine in diamond beauty. First, is our attitude. Going back to one of our key verses on salvation at the beginning of this chapter, Psalm 149:4 tells us that "the

Lord takes pleasure in His people; He will beautify the humble with salvation."

The key attitude in order for this beautification process to happen is humility. Humility begins when we stand in the full truth and light of who we actually are realizing the true extent of God's mercy to us. Humility helps us fully realize we are only saved as a gift of God! "By grace you have been saved through faith, and that not of yourselves; it is the gift of God not of works, lest anyone should boast." (Ephesians 2:8,9)

True humility brings the realization that we are completely dependent on what Christ has done for us, and not on what we can do for Him or in ourselves. The apostle Peter tells women, "Do not let your adornment be merely outward—arranging the hair, wearing gold, or putting on fine apparel— rather let it be the hidden person of the heart, with the incorruptible beauty of a gentle and quiet spirit, which is very precious in the sight of God."(1 Peter 3:3-4). The gentle and quiet spirit that he speaks about is not about a subdued personality, it is literally about being full of peace because of having total confidence and dependence in who God is and how He works in your life. The word gentle in that verse is praus in the Greek (Strong's #4235 and 4239) which literally means a humility that is meek—it is power under perfect control. The power comes from your absolute confidence that God has your back no matter what your circumstances. That brings peace in your words and actions. Peter was not talking about weak women, he was talking about women who are so confident that they can sit back and relax.

Jesus models what humility looks like for us as we walk in salvation:

"And being found in appearance as a man, he humbled himself by becoming obedient to death—even death on a cross!...Do everything without grumbling or arguing, so that you may become blameless and pure, children of God without fault in a warped and crooked generation. Then you will shine among them like stars in the sky." (Philippians 2:5-15 NIV)

God wants you to shine as stars in the darkness of the world around you, and one of the ways to do that is to follow Jesus' example of humility and submission rather than the world's example of grumbling or arguing. Which brings me to the second point to understand in our redemption which is that we choose to do life God's way, and not ours.

Even though he was the apostle known for his love, John's words might seem harsh in our church culture today. He says, "If someone claims, "I know God," but doesn't obey God's commandments, that person is a liar and is not living in the truth," (I John 2:4). James goes on to set the bar for believers "therefore, to him who knows to do good and does not do it, to him it is sin," (James 4:17).

You have to obey God's commands and direction, rather than doing what is right in your own eyes. One of the most tragic examples of this concept in the Old Testament is King Saul. He only partially obeyed what the prophet Samuel told him was clearly God's will, and he defended it rather than repenting when Samuel explained the issue. In 1 Samuel 15, Saul couldn't understand why what he was doing was so bad. Samuel rebuked him, explaining that obedience was better than sacrifice and that obedience is what the Lord delights in. He added that being in rebellion against God is as witchcraft—serving the devil. Then he explains stubbornness (persisting in disobedience) was the same as sin and idolatry (1 Samuel 15:22, 23). Why? Because our sacrifices are what we are willing to do for God. They are our plan for obedience, retaining our own lordship of our lives, making it our call. Obedience is lining up with God's plan for your life.

Making excuses for following your own ways and caring more about what others think than what God thinks is a characteristic of someone who is kidding themselves about their commitment to God. Saul's response to Samuel's charge was "I have sinned, for I transgressed the commandment of the Lord and your words because I feared the people and obeyed their voice. Now therefore, please pardon my sin, and return with me, that I may worship the Lord" (V. 24, 25) That might have sounded good at first, but Saul had no real remorse for rejecting God, just a desire to be forgiven so life could go on as usual. He was not willing to deal with any consequences. Instead he became angry and justified himself when anyone tried to speak to him about wrong choices.

That's called "cheap grace" as Dietrich Bonhoeffer (1906-1945), a German theologian and martyr, coined it. Cheap grace is easily asked for and received because a person who wants it feels they can do anything they want as God will forgive them—after all, if He is a loving God, He has to, right? Because of cheap grace, many expect God to keep blessing them no matter how they respond to Him or live. Bonhoeffer writes that cheap grace will always justify the sin rather than the sinner.

I have a friend who desperately wanted to get married. She was still single in her early 50s and was on several dating sites. She believes in God and can be found at Mass in her Catholic church several times a week. When her most recent relationship blew up, she called me lamenting that God had not answered her prayers (again!) and that she could not reconcile her devotion to a loving God with her lack of success in this area of her life. After a lengthy conversation, she confessed she had slept with this man but she had immediately gone to Confession. I had to gently remind her of this truth—God prefers obedience over sacrifice. She knew the right thing to do, but she chose her own path and then immediately asked for forgiveness. Of course, the forgiveness was granted, but she was no closer to her answered prayer.

What does it take to turn the whole thing around? Simple: true repentance and sincere obedience. That was the reason God could forgive David for his grievous sin, but Saul never walked in God's grace again. David was ready to do whatever it took. He cried out "wash me!" (Psalm 51:7). That washing was the type of washing in those days where the clothes would be beaten against the rocks until all dirt was loosened, it was not a pleasant soaking in a warm tub. David begged God, "Do not cast me away from Your presence, and do not take your Holy Spirit from me!" (Psalm 51:11). As soon as we confess our sin with godly sorrow (2 Cor 7:10), God is just to forgive it (Rom 10:9, Jn. 1:9). He will never despise or reject a contrite heart (Psalm 51:16,17). God will be right there for you, and none of "those who trust in Him shall be condemned!" (Psalm 34:22). Jesus explained that to "abide" or stay in His love, we must obey His commandments (John 15:10).

God will love us no matter what, but He is completely just and if we refuse Him, He will let us have our way based on our own will. (Matt 7:21-23) Let's receive the full benefits of God's love—eternal life, joy, peace—as we obey Him so we can attain diamond beauty and reflect His glory as we live our lives.

4) God "crowns us with lovingkindness and tender mercies" (Psalm 103:4 NKJ)

The fourth restoration benefit of salvation is that you are crowned with the state of God's continual lovingkindness and mercy. God's mercy (racham, Strong's #7355) or compassion is based on His lovingkindness (hesed, Strong's #2618). Hesed is the covenant loyalty and commitment God demonstrates to His people. It combines the promises of total commitment, acceptance, and support for all eternity. This is a characteristic of God towards His bride and children. Understanding God's lovingkindness is central to living an abundant life because when we grasp the commitment and loyalty we now have as part of our inheritance, it helps us radiate confidence and strength.

Picture God looking down from heaven and saying, "I see every flaw and all the ways you fail, and I am completely committed to you anyway. I look at you with total love and acceptance just as a Father adores and loves His little child, even when she messes up. My love, strength and compassion will be with you every day for the rest of your life." He showers lovingkindness on His daughters because we belong to Him. It is a special blessing of our position as His own chosen people (Matt 5:45, 1 Peter 2:9).

Thomas Brooks, a Puritan writer, says: "Divine favour (hesed) is better than life(Ps 63:3); it is better than life with all its revenues, with all its appurtenances, as honours, riches, pleasures, applause, etc.; yea, it is better than many lives put together. Now you know at what a high-rate men value their lives; they will bleed, sweat, vomit, purge, part with an estate, yea, with a limb, yea, limbs, to preserve their lives... Many men have been weary of their lives, as is evident in Scripture and history; but no man was ever yet found that was weary of the love and favour (hesed) of God."[17]

Here's a list of the blessings of Lovingkindness for you:

- God's lovingkindness preserves us:

"Do not withhold Your tender mercies from me, O Lord; Let Your lovingkindness and Your truth continually preserve me." (Psalm 40:11)

- It revives us:

"Revive me according to Your lovingkindness, So that I may keep the testimony of Your mouth." (Psalm 119:88)

"Hear my voice according to Your lovingkindness; O Lord, revive me according to Your justice." (Psalm 119:149)

"Consider how I love Your precepts; Revive me, O Lord, according to Your lovingkindness." (Psalm 119:159)

- God commands it and delights in it as part of His covenant faithfulness:

"The Lord will command His lovingkindness in the daytime, And in the night His song shall be with me— A prayer to the God of my life." (Psalm 42:8)

"Nevertheless My lovingkindness I will not utterly take from him, Nor allow My faithfulness to fail." (Psalm 89:33)

"But let him who glories glory in this, That he understands and knows Me, That I am the Lord, exercising lovingkindness, judgment, and righteousness in the earth. For in these I delight," says the Lord. (Jeremiah 9:24)

- It blots out our sins

" Have mercy upon me, O God, According to Your lovingkindness; According to the multitude of Your tender mercies, Blot out my transgressions." (Psalm 51:1)

David ends Psalm 23 with the certainty of knowing our God sent His mercy and goodness as blessings that would actually pursue Him. It is not enough for God to just let all that goodness and mercy sit there, waiting for you, He has them pursue you.

"Surely goodness and mercy(hesed) shall follow me all the days of my life; and I will dwell in the house of the Lord forever."

As a woman becomes confident and secure in God's lovingkindness, she will radiate diamond beauty to the world.

5) "Who satisfies your mouth with good things, so that your youth is renewed like the eagle's" (Psalm 103:5).

David saved the best for last as far as I am concerned, in this youth conscious age! At first glance, this verse tells the believer God will restore to them the energy and vitality comparable to that of an eagle. Sounds good right? I will take any renewing of youth God has to give. But that is just the tip of the iceberg. Let's study what God is saying specifically.

The bird here is actually the griffon vulture, which David and the other Old Testament writers would have been familiar with in their part of the world. The idea of a vulture being a bird we would want to emulate is a strange one if we are not familiar with it. The griffon was considered to be a majestic bird whose image was used as an idol to represent the god-like power of pagan nations, such as Assyria and Egypt, which surrounded Israel.

The griffon has many characteristics that make it the perfect, desirable model of strength and renewal. It flies higher and sees more keenly than any other bird. A griffon can fly up to 36,000 feet, the height at which jets fly, and it will typically fly for 6-7 hours a day which is why many scholars cross reference this verse with Isaiah 40:31:

"But those who wait on the Lord shall renew their strength; they shall mount up with wings like eagles, they shall run and not be weary, they shall walk and not faint."

The griffon is in a continual renewal process that changes as the bird matures, and never stops. Each year it molts or sheds old or damaged feathers which are replaced with new ones. When I was looking at various pictures of the molting process, I couldn't help but smile as I noticed that as the bird gets older, the feathers are smoother and shinier and actually make him look softer and more attractive than the younger version. It reminded me of the way saintly older women, with the love of Jesus shining in their eyes, are softer and gentler than their younger selves, making the world a kinder place and making people smile from the encouragement of just being around them. In God's plan, people want to be around you more as you get older, rather than discarding you because your usefulness and physical appeal has faded.

The renewal of molting requires an enormous amount of energy for which the griffon needs a tremendous amount of nourishment. It will eat and eat until it is literally glutted to the point it has a hard time flying. This is why the first part of Psalm 103:5 is so amazingly appropriate. God wants to fill us with good things, to the point of overflowing, to renew our strength and shed off the old worldly us, leaving no room for anything that's not of Him. He knows change requires a lot of energy, and wants to fill us with what will give us the strength to be able to do it.

Let's look at this verse word for word in the Hebrew:

Sabea: When God satisfies (sabea, Strong's #7645) our mouth, the word here literally means He fills us to the fullest, in excess and abundance.

Adi: The word "mouth" (adi, Strong's #5716) literally means an ornament with which one is decked, or an adornment, a jewel. Here it is used in the feminine form which also indicates age or maturity. Many translations use the wording "your necessities or desires or life" for mouth. That is multi-level filling! Here we are being told we are a jewel, God is filling us with what we perfectly need for our age or maturity level, and He is filling our personal desires.

Tob and Dabar: What are the good things (tob, Strong's #2896 and dabar Strong's #1697)? They are literally translated as bountiful, beautiful, agreeable words, counsels, or promises.

Chadash: The word renew (chadash, Strong's #2318) is literally to be rebuilt or made fresh.

When we put it all together, this verse is actually saying: God is filling you, His jewel, and all your desires, which are precious ornaments with which He is decking you out, to the fullest point you can contain, with the promises, direction, and counsel you need as a woman at your age and maturity level, so you can be rebuilt and refreshed and soar like the griffon, a noble, strong bird who flies the highest and longest of all birds!

Are you leaping in your spirit right now as you let God's goodness towards you settle in? I was when I began to understand this precious benefit for His daughters. We are his jewel that he makes beautiful and able to soar with strength.

Paul said, "Therefore we do not lose heart. Even though our outward man is perishing, yet the inward man is being renewed day by day. For our light affliction, which is but for a moment, is working for us a far more exceeding and eternal weight of glory" (2 Cor 4;16-17). The word "renewed" Paul uses here is the same term that David implies meaning freshness as applied to someone's age.

There are other verses that give us the same promises of vitality and freshness even in our old age, most notably Psalm 1:3:

"He shall be like a tree, planted by the rivers of water, that brings forth its fruit in its season, whose leaf also shall not wither; and whatever he does shall prosper."

And Psalm 92:13,14:

"Those who are planted in the house of the Lord shall flourish in the courts of our God. They shall still bear fruit in old age; they shall be fresh and flourishing."

In God, there is much less fear around aging because we are maturing in humility and wisdom and being proven in character. For most of us, when we are "advanced in years," we are advancing in the "good things" of God. Abraham was 100, and Sarah was 90 when Isaac was born; Caleb was 80 when he began to fight for his inheritance in Canaan; Moses was 80 when he began his new career as deliverer of Israel; Zechariah and Elizabeth were described as old and "well advanced in years" (Luke 1:18) when Gabriel appeared and told them they would have John the Baptist, the greatest of men "to be born of women" until that time (Matt 11:11). Those are just a few who were just getting started accomplishing God's main purposes for them and seeing their promises fulfilled as they aged.

If you are still breathing, which I am assuming you are since you are reading this, then God will continue to satisfy "your mouth (your necessity and desire at your personal age and situation) with good' (AMP) so you can walk in all the "good works" (Philippians 1:6) God has prepared for you (Ephesians 2:10) decked out with God's diamond beauty, blessed, a woman of excellence, your "value far above rubies.(Proverbs 31:10).

God institutes His Inside-out Beauty Plan through the restoration process of salvation because of His pleasure in us as His beloved (Psalm 149:4). No matter what state you were born into, as you live in salvation, God restores and beautifies you to become a brilliant reflection of His glory. He takes the negatives in you and replaces them with positives resulting in an abundant, radiant life.

Chapter 4
How the Devil Has Twisted God's Plan

I hate to spend any time focusing on the devil, but the world, under the devil's influence, has taken God's Inside-Out plan and twisted it to become the Outside-In plan. Instead of abundant life, the thief, as Jesus referred to him, came to "steal, kill and destroy" our joy, peace, and confidence (John 10:10). How has he done this? In three important ways:

By Getting us to Conform to the World

The devil is not omnipotent (all powerful) or omnipresent (able to be everywhere at the same time) the way God is. This means he has limited power and time to carry out as much destruction as he can. He has to use his limited resources to reach as many people as quickly as possible. He has inundated us through technology and the media with focus on our outside, so we are defined by weight, body curves, skin perfection, and well applied make-up. Girls and women of all ages are miserable as they compare themselves to idealized images that are impossible to live up to except in perfect conditions—even for the models that perpetuate the images! If the models can only look perfect when air-brushed or given special spa treatments that smooth over skin imperfections for only a few hours for their photo shoots and runway shows, how do we attain that in our "regular" lives? The answer is we can't. As we try to conform to the world's image of beauty, it robs us of our confidence.

Most women don't say "that's a fairy-tale image it's not real" and walk away. Instead, we say (even subconsciously), "I am pathetic because I can't look like that myself." It is even harder for little girls who have a difficult time separating any of what they see from reality. No wonder 80% of women are dissatisfied with their appearance, and tweens are putting on firming cream!

Even though people in advertising admit that the images are photo-shopped, and they put different women's body parts together or reshape the parts to form the illusions, we still look at them and let the ideals define our perceptions of ourselves. This is deception and women live in it like never before because it is all around them. Deception is defined as a trick, a fraud, something that is intended to deceive[18] and it is the devil's specialty.

Our eyes determine what we let into our minds and thoughts. Luke 11:34 says "the lamp of the body is the eye. Therefore when your eye is good (healthy), your whole body is full of light." Jesus means that our eye has to be able to perceive what is actually true in order to be healthy and moving in the right direction. What we look at and focus on concerning the images of beauty affects our thoughts and therefore our attitudes. It can make our eyes see in an unhealthy manner. That is why Jesus warns in Luke 11:35 "therefore take heed (be careful) that the light which is in you is not darkness."

It takes an active effort to keep our eyes off of the images we are assaulted with every day so as not to get consumed with them. Peter tells us to "Be sober (self-controlled), be vigilant; because your adversary the devil walks about like a roaring lion, seeking whom he may devour" (1 Peter 5:8). Solomon advises that we keep our hearts with all diligence because out of it spring the issues of life" (Proverbs 4:23). The enemy wants us to conform our minds to these images without a thought, so they become what we associate with beauty. When this happens, our "light," or eyes, actually lead us to accepting darkness as truth.

When the church is an imitation of the world, there is a problem. We were never called to conform to the world, but we are called, as Paul says, to be transformed by the renewing of our minds (Romans 12:2). This transformation is designed to restore us to see our beauty through God's standards of individuality which gives us confidence rather than robbing us of it.

By Deceiving us to Conform to Church Legalism

Another way the enemy implements the Outside-In Plan is to make "religious" people use outside appearances as the determinant of what makes a woman holy. Women have been the object of the enemy's wrath since Genesis (Genesis 3:15). Legalism in religious practice puts women in bondage—no make-up, no jewelry, only certain clothing and hairstyles! Thank goodness God looks at our hearts and potential, rather than the outside. Mary Magdalene would definitely have been stoned if legalism was God's way of dealing with women. When he looked at this adulterous woman, possessed by seven demons, head and eyes down (as is so typical of young women that live in shame and rejection), He saw her heart and how love and acceptance could change and free her. This was so opposite of the Pharisees and scribes—the church of that day (John 8:3-11)—who lived in rules and standards that entrapped them in self-righteousness.

If God had a problem with women being adorned with jewelry and fine clothing, then Ezekiel's prophetic description of how God dressed His own wife, Israel in Ez. 16:10-13 would have to be completely discounted. God described in those verses in detail how He showed His love for Israel by how He "dressed" her:

"I clothed you in embroidered cloth and gave you sandals of badger skin; I clothed you with fine linen and covered you with silk. I adorned you with ornaments, put bracelets on your wrists, and a chain on your neck. And I put a jewel in your nose, earrings in your ears, and a beautiful crown on your head. Thus you were adorned with gold and silver, and your clothing was of fine linen, silk, and embroidered cloth." NKJV

God doesn't have a problem with women receiving the best of beauty treatments, either. Esther was in the middle of His providential plan for her to become Queen when she was undergoing 12 months of beauty preparations (Esther 2:12). Think about what that might look like today, if you were in the beauty pageant of your life thrown by the richest man on earth looking for his new wife. The show, The Bachelor, pales in comparison. Esther was just as much in the middle of God's will as Joseph was during his 13 years in slavery and prison to become second in command in Egypt (Genesis 39:20, Psalm 105:18-22). Both had the same commission: to save their people from extinction.

But the arguments continue: We shouldn't be focused on make up or fancy clothes, right? Or are you arguing the point that as God's people, we should be an example of the best? After all, there was Esther and Solomon in all his glory and prosperity and so on and so on. That means we should be well-dressed and have all the latest technology at our disposal to present the best possible selves we can, right? Yes to both.

It all really comes down to faith and obedience. A careful reading of Romans 14 and 15:1-7 explains the godly way to handle the differences. Whatever you cannot do in good conscience and in faith is sin to you. That is really a personal choice and standard, though. If wearing earrings or lipstick makes you feel that you are not obeying the convictions God has impressed on you, don't do it. Even though there is no specific prohibition in the Word about it, it is important to obey the things God is calling you to do as an individual, but don't judge others to the same standard. That is what the Pharisees did with the very Son of God, calling him a sinner because of the company he kept and what he ate and drank because of their strict interpretations of godliness. Live according to your faith. Only you and God know why it might be smarter for you to abstain or practice certain standards. Our faith and walk is ours alone before God. Here, again, is your uniqueness. He fashioned your heart individually (Psa. 33:15).

Years ago, I went to the Ukraine to teach at a church leadership training school. While there, I asked about getting my nails done as we had some time off at the end of the week. The interpreter told me she couldn't recommend a salon because it was against the church's conviction to get nails painted, and she didn't know of any places. Surprised, I asked if they had noticed I had polish on my nails and if that was a stumbling block for them. She replied the church was used to American ministers coming who wore a lot of makeup or pants or nail polish because we were so used to compromise in that area in the American church, so they made an allowance for it. I was shocked. They felt that they were living a higher standard of holiness because of their convictions about women's dress and make-up.

Were they weaker or holier? That is really God's call because only He knows their hearts. Romans 14:3,4 NKJV says, "Let not him who eats despise him who does not eat, and let not him who does not eat judge him who eats; for God has received him. Who are you to judge another's servant? To his own master he stands or falls. Indeed, he will be made to stand, for God is able to make him stand." I spent the rest of the week with my hands in my pockets because we weren't in a place where I could easily get nail polish remover. I didn't want to make my sisters stumble in this area of freedom in my own life (Rom. 14:21-22; Rom. 15:2). From their perspective, they were trying to live Romans 15:1 "bearing with the scruples of the weak," which was the way they saw my "American" standards.

The enemy has a clever plan here. Some women can feel condemned, others, justified, by their own works rather than by their faith and relationship with Jesus. The church can continue to walk in self-righteousness rather than love and grace, feeling justified as the Pharisees and scribes did with Jesus. One for the devil, zero for the saints.

The added bonus of division in the body of Christ as we argue or break fellowship over how we should look makes our witness to the world weak. Two for the devil, and still zero for the saints. God's desire is for us to "receive one another as Christ also received us, to the glory of God" (Rom. 15:7). That is when the world will know we belong to Jesus —when we love each other despite our different standards and leave the judgment to God (John 13:35).

By Deceiving Us through Distorted Mindsets

The enemy knows the battlefield is in our mind, so he tries to distort our perceptions of femininity. Distorted "mindsets" affect the way we perceive and even want to view ourselves as beautiful women. Some of these distorted mindsets are:

The Damaged Mindset of Abuse

Some women have been hurt and abused by men and they do not want to be beautiful. In their mind, the goal or result of beauty is to attract men and men are evil, hurtful creatures. Maybe in the twisted way they were treated, the men even blamed them for the abuse because of how they looked. If they can give men fewer reasons to like them or notice them, they feel safer.

These women tend to see other women who are feminine (or want to be beautiful) as weak. Weakness is pain, and they are determined to protect themselves from this type of pain at all costs. Unfortunately, they have traded one type of pain for another. For these women, even bringing up the subject of femininity stirs up reactionary wrath because it touches an open wound that never properly healed. The pain many women have suffered is heartbreaking and Jesus (a man) alone understands all of it because he took every ounce of pain when He suffered on the cross. Our Messiah and Lord knows this pain intimately. Isaiah 53:3-5, NKJV, speaks of someone who was "despised and rejected— a man of sorrows, acquainted with deepest grief. We turned our backs on him and looked the other way. He was despised, and we did not care. Yet it was our weaknesses he carried; it was our sorrows that weighed him down. And we thought his troubles were a punishment from God, a punishment for his own sins! But he was pierced for our rebellion, crushed for our sins. He was beaten so we could be whole. He was whipped so we could be healed."

The Message version of this same verse says, "a man who suffered, who knew pain firsthand. One look at him and people turned away. We looked down on him, thought he was scum. But the fact is, it was our pains he carried— our disfigurements, all the things wrong with us. We thought he brought it on himself, that God was punishing him for his own failures. But it was our sins that did that to him, that ripped and tore and crushed him— our sins! He took the punishment, and that made us whole. Through his bruises we get healed."

Maybe you can relate to how no one cared for Him and His pain. Maybe you felt blamed even though you were totally innocent in what happened to you. Maybe you thought God was punishing you. Maybe you have felt that you were ripped and crushed by other people's sins. He bore your sorrows (mental, physical and spiritual) so you don't have to spend your life carrying them. Let Him carry them. Lay them down, along with the hatred and anger that kept you prisoner. Paul says in Hebrews 4:15 about Jesus, "This High Priest of ours understands our weaknesses, for he faced all of the same testings we do, yet he did not sin." What was His heart toward his abusers and revilers? "Father, forgive them" (Luke 23:34). He handed his pain to the Father and prayed for their forgiveness. Jesus understands your desire to give in to and live in hate and anger. But He chose not to. We can do the same, because in the next verse it says, "So let us come boldly to the throne of our gracious God. There we will receive his mercy, and we will find grace to help us when we need it most."(Heb. 4:16) You can access Him whenever you need to and cry out for help to overcome your hatred and pain and be free. The word "boldly" is translated in Greek as "totally honest without reservations." We can do this because God alone totally gets our pain and hurt.

I know we touched on forgiveness in the last chapter, but I want to add to your understanding here. Forgiveness is critical because Jesus said that if we hate our brother, then we are condemned just as a murderer is condemned (Matt 5:21). This seems harsh on the surface because many people feel justified by the horror of what they have experienced to hate their brother (or father, or neighbor). Jesus said this, however, because hating our brother is murdering him in our hearts. Every time we even say our brother is a fool, we are hurting him/her. The call of a follower of Jesus is to love our enemies (Matt 5:43-47). Evil can never overcome evil; it just increases the evil flying around. Only love and mercy can overcome hatred and anger and neutralize it. In

Romans 12:17-21, Paul lays out how we should treat our enemies refusing vengeance, admonishing us to "not be overcome by evil, but overcome evil with good." The only way to stop the pain is to render it dead by obedience to the laws of love and mercy, just as Jesus did through the cross.

As a therapist, I have had the honor of watching girls who had spent years with abusive foster parents or family members healed through giving their pain to God and choosing forgiveness. One girl had been physically and emotionally abused for almost 10 years, and yet, she could look me in the eye and express sadness and pity for the abuser because she had forgiven him as a result of her relationship with Jesus. Her greatest hope was that after her abuser came out of prison, he would know the Lord and be changed, but she was free. She was excited about her life and her future. There was a beauty in her that her salvation restored. No amount of the world's beauty treatments could have come close to achieving that result. She was an example of diamond beauty.

Note: On Forgiveness

I want to explain here that I am speaking of walking in forgiveness from a place of safety and not staying in an abusive situation. There is never a time when staying in a violent situation should be done because you want to walk in love. Usually the cycle of pain and violence cannot be broken until the living arrangement changes. In those situations, the most loving thing you can do is leave, so the other person has the opportunity to change and/or so you can heal. Jesus himself advised "Don't give holy things to depraved men. Don't give pearls to swine! They will trample the pearls and turn and attack you." (Matt 7:6 TLB) You as God's child are holy and should not give yourself to anyone who is abusive (depraved).

The Deceived Mindset of One Beauty Standard

Did you ever think it strange that a friend would find someone—guy or girl—attractive when you didn't? That has happened several times to me with men and women friends. Someone will comment, "Wow that girl is pretty!" and I'll think "really?" Or I will see a girl and say she is beautiful, and it will puzzle my husband or friend.

Ever wonder why that happens? Because God made each of us to be a unique masterpiece. Physical beauty defies a set definition. Different people have different attractions. One loves Picasso, another would rather stare at a Monet. Both are priceless.

One of the lies the enemy wants women to believe is that we must look a certain way to be beautiful. The reality is there is no "certain way" that makes one more attractive than another. The old adage that beauty is in the eye of the beholder is just as relevant today as ever, but we have pushed it aside and bought the idea that we must have a certain body type. For women with this distorted mindset, the body type is almost certainly not the one the woman has—it is always one that is unattainable or just out of her reach. She becomes trapped into feeling like she is doomed to be unhappy because she is ugly. She might even fall into self-pity, feeling that somehow she was cheated. The enemy loves for us to meditate on whatever is a distorted truth, "whatever things are trivial, whatever things are unjust, whatever things are impure, whatever things are not lovely, whatever things are of bad report, if there is any deficiency and if there is anything unpraiseworthy." That is the devil's plan—the exact opposite of what Paul wrote in Phil 4:8 when he exhorted us to "meditate on these things."

The enemy knows the feeling of beauty actually comes from an inner confidence in becoming who God has made us to be, which is why women can feel beautiful at any age. He wants us to feel trapped and dissatisfied so we do not trust God's plan. He knows if we grasp hold of the truth that we all have unique beauty that God wants to develop into our best selves and "do exceedingly abundantly above all that we ask or think, according to the power that works in us" (Ephesians 3:20 NKJV) then we will be set free from envy and self-pity. He certainly doesn't want us running after God's best for us. He would much rather have you try to be an imitation of someone else because then you won't be submitting to the Master's hand forming you into His masterpiece. Accepting one beauty standard traps you in envy, coveting someone else's beauty. God wants to free you of envy.

In Psalm 73, when the psalmist went into the sanctuary (God's presence), he realized the truth about the envy he was feeling toward people who seemed like they had what he wanted. That is when his foolishness hits him. "Thus my heart was grieved and I was vexed (pierced) in my mind." (V. 21). The source of the grief was that he is telling God by his discontent that what God gave him wasn't enough and therefore God, Himself, was not good or enough. The enemy loves when he can get us to believe a lie about God and charge Him with wrong.

The psalmist realizes he actually has the best part because he has his God. "I was so foolish and ignorant; I was like a beast before You. Nevertheless, I am continually with You; You hold me by my right hand. You will guide me with Your counsel and afterward receive me to glory. Whom have I in heaven but You? And there is none upon earth that I desire besides You. My flesh and my heart fail, But God is the strength of my heart and my portion forever." (Psalm 73:22-26) The psalmist decides he will trust God's counsel! He sets his desire on God and lets God be the strength of his heart, knowing it is good (tob, Strong's #2896) meaning beautiful, to "draw near to God" (Psalm 73:28).

Prov. 31: 29-31 NKJ also tells us the end of the story when we choose to go for diamond beauty: "Many daughters have done well, but you excel them all. Charm is deceitful and (physical) beauty is passing, but a woman who fears the Lord, she shall be praised. Give her of the fruit of her hands, and let her own works praise her in the gates."

Even when the enemy tries to twist it, God's tried and true methods of diamond beauty will always prevail, even over technology! Just turn on the TV and look at some of the older ladies who refused to age gracefully and made outward beauty their idol. Their accomplishments and abilities are overshadowed by their vanity which they wear on their frozen, unnatural faces for the world to see. How different for a woman of God whose "own works will praise her in the gates." She will be respected and remembered for what she has done because of who she is. True confidence, value and honor come from attaining beauty from the inside-out, not the outside-in.

Part II:
The Beauty Treatments

Chapter 5
The Water Treatments

So far, we've been like a griffon vulture flying around and getting the overview of what God wants to do in each of our lives. Now it's time to zero in on the things we need to "apply" to renew us. It is time to go to God's "spa" and have some work done.

When we go to a great spa, known for rejuvenating and beautifying, we have to be stripped down and cleansed before anything is added. All impurities are washed off so the treatments applied afterward can be completely absorbed and benefit us in the best way. Spiritually, God does the same thing. Let's talk about three essential water treatments God wants us to apply to ourselves to bring out our beauty.

Water Treatment #1

The first treatment is called water baptism. You may be familiar with water baptism, but let's do a deeper dive into the significance of this event in every Christian's life, and how it ties to restoration. In Ezekiel 16 God prophetically recounts how He had chosen Israel to be His beloved bride and how He turned her into a legendary beauty and the envy of all nations. In the passage, the first thing God does after He finds Israel abandoned and left to die is to thoroughly wash her from what is still clinging to her (remnants of where she has come from—her old life). "I bathed you with water and washed the blood from you and put ointments on you." (Ezekiel 16:9 NKJV) In the early church, Christians were baptized as soon as they believed and repented.

The apostle Paul explains the significance of baptism:

"Or do you not know that as many of us as were baptized into Christ were baptized into His death? Therefore, we were buried with Him through baptism into death, that just as Christ was raised from the dead by the glory of the Father, even so we also should walk in newness of life. For if we have been united together in the likeness of His death, certainly we also shall be in the likeness of His resurrection, knowing this, that our old man was crucified with Him, that the body of sin might be done away with, that we should no longer be slaves of sin. For he that has died is free from sin." (Romans 6:3-7 NKJV)

Water baptism is our identification with Christ's death and our public commitment to Him as the one who died as our substitute. It is our public statement that we are dead to our old life. The best part, though, is that we do not stay down in death, but are lifted up again. Baptism is the visible symbol of stripping off the old nature and putting on the new so you can walk in resurrection life. The word resurrection in the verse above literally means restoration of life and recovery of truth. (Strong's #386)

Even though water baptism is modeled and commanded by Jesus and prominent in the New Testament (see Mark 16:16), God set the water baptism precedent back in Exodus (see Ex. 14:21-31) when He symbolically started with water as His first act of salvation as the Israelites began their journey. God had Moses lead them from their old life through the Red Sea to the abundant life He had waiting for them in the promised land. As they came up out of the Red Sea, even though they did not technically get wet, they looked back and saw the enemies that held them captive all those years die. They watched them get buried and left under the water. God had completely delivered them and they were saved once and for all. The chapter on their old life was closed for good. That is a physical picture of what happens to us spiritually as we get water baptized. Our old self is dead and we are walking in newness—our new life in Christ. It signifies and confirms that we are entering a new journey with God. When people are hesitant to get water baptized, it is usually a sign that they are not ready to close the door on their old life, and publicly declare their commitment.

When the Jews were scattered outside of Israel after the Babylonian captivity, numerous Gentiles sought admission to Israel, wanting to become Jews. The required public repentance and acceptance of Mosaic Law was accompanied by immersion in water, which symbolized total cleansing from the defilements of pagan religions. That is why in the New Testament, John's water baptism and later the early church custom needed little explanation. It was a Jewish common practice for centuries.

Baptism is a fundamental aspect of Christianity, yet today, many churches have gotten away from the emphasis the early church placed on baptizing new converts right away. There are few requirements the

New Testament sets down to walk in the Christian life. In fact, there are only two: repentance and baptism. It is important to commit yourself publicly as soon as possible after you make the choice to live for Him.

Water Treatment #2

After God washes you through baptism, He continues to clean you and then equip you as you learn to apply His Word to your life:

"How can a young man cleanse his way? By taking heed according to Your word."(Psalm 119:9 NKJV)

"Husbands, love your wives, even as Christ also loved the church, and gave Himself for her to make her holy, cleansing her by the *washing with water* through the word" (Ephesians 5:25,26 NKJV).

How does the Word of God cleanse us? Paul says:

"For the word of God is living and powerful and sharper than any two-edged sword, piercing even to the division of soul and spirit, and of joints and marrow, and is a discerner of the thoughts and intents of the heart" (Hebrews 4:12 NKJV).

The Word of God is a powerful, active, and effective cleansing agent that changes us. God's Word helps us separate and judge our thoughts and attitudes according to His standards, which are pure and true. This discernment enables us to see our thoughts and actions for what they really are. When we see the truth and understand how we need to change to live in it, we are set free from our old mindsets and begin to grow in a positive, healthy way. It transforms the way we think, then feel, then act--that good old CBT triangle referred to in Chapter 2--which ultimately affects the way we shine in the world.

God's Word helps us discern not only what is inside of us, but also what is around us. David said in Psalm 119:105, "Your word is a lamp to my feet and a light to my path." The Word equips you to understand what path you should walk by providing the information on how to do it so you can walk securely.

God's Word, which washes us clean, is our guide and map to stay on the path or highway of the race we are running as Christians. It is the complete training manual and rule book on how to run it to win. God has a path that He will illuminate for you where, if you stay on it, the devil, the "roaring lion" (1 Peter 5:8), cannot hurt you. The enemy has no access to this highway. It is out of his reach. What is the name of the path or highway that we need to stay on as Christians? It is called The Highway of Holiness:

Isaiah 35:8-9 NKJV says, "A highway shall be there, and a road, and it shall be called the Highway of Holiness. The unclean shall not pass over it, but it shall be for others. Whoever walks the road, although a fool, shall not go astray. No lion shall be there, Nor shall any ravenous beast go up on it; It shall not be found there. But the redeemed shall walk there."

In California, there are some high elevations in different mountain ranges. We also have some nasty snakes including rattlesnakes. But I find it amazing that once you get to a certain elevation above the timberline, there are no longer snakes. They can't live there. You no longer have to worry about an attack. I want to live above the timberline spiritually, and stay on the Highway of Holiness where I am out of reach of the devil.

Another fact I love about this path is that Isaiah says even if you are a fool, you will not go astray. That is a powerful promise for me since I do not always make the best choices. His Word is a way to live that will keep us on a path that is straight and safe. It is such a freeing thing to be able to count on God's path when this world is so full of choices and paths that are not safe, even if they seem good at first. Proverbs 16:25 NKJV says, "There is a way that seems right to a man, But its end is the way of death."

That was especially true for me with men. I would meet a guy that I thought really liked me and many times it would end up being a short lived, "just trying to get into my pants" experience. As I surrendered my life and let God's word become my standard, and I became determined to stay on the Highway of Holiness, I found that it spared me a lot of pain. Guys that were only interested in using me lost interest quickly when they realized I was serious about staying pure. Many times, a man would find it really intriguing that I had such high moral standards, and some would even test me and try to be the one that I would give into. But if they just wanted a good time, it would be a relatively quick decision to end the relationship when I stuck to my resolve. I found that to be a big safeguard for me.

One of the biggest thieves that steals beauty for a woman is giving her precious self to a man who does not value her or tosses her aside. That makes a woman lose her self-worth a little piece at a time. The message we keep hearing in our culture is that our sexuality is meant to be used for our pleasure and it's ridiculous to not sleep with men whenever we feel like it. We are told we have just as much right to do that as a man does. Yes, we do, but this completely ignores the deeper psychological need women have to be cherished and pursued.

Think about that for yourself. I know I never feel more beautiful than when a man is actively cherishing and pursuing me. That is not just a personal opinion, either. Through my work as a counselor and church leader, I have spoken to hundreds of women and wives where that is the deepest longing in a relationship. That does not happen in a relationship that becomes sexual quickly, because sex becomes the foundational way men relate to you. They have not had the time to get to know you as a whole person. Then it feels like the water gets muddy because many men keep the sex front and center in the interactions. Women want to be heard and valued, and for sex to be the expression of that, not the basis for it.

Proverbs 3:5-6 (NKJV) says, "Trust in the Lord with all your heart, and lean not on your own understanding; In all your ways acknowledge Him, and He shall direct your paths." In these verses God is promising you to make a path that is straight, right, and pleasing. Let God cleanse you by thorough washing, and equip yourself by knowing His book of truth inside and out so you can run safely on the holiness path and get that prize: your diamond beauty.

Water Treatment #3

In certain places in the world there are therapeutic spas that people will travel to for the healing properties of the water. These waters provide a level of benefit that reaches deep down to the inside of a weary or sick person where healing change flows. The waters enable the soaker to function on a new level of life and vitality. The next water treatment is His Presence, the Living Water, the source of all healing and refreshing. In this next level of water treatment, we need to stay and soak for a while to experience the benefits.

God gives us a picture of His healing waters in Ez. 47:1-12. Please take a moment and read it through before you go any further in the chapter. The first thing that is important to notice in this passage is the source of this water. In verse 1 God takes Ezekiel to the door of the temple, the place where God dwells. To get in the water we have to go to where it is, which means we must go to Jesus who is the source, the Living Water Himself. But not only is Jesus the Living Water, He is also the Word made Flesh (John 1:1). The relationship of the presence and word of God come perfectly together in the life and sacrifice of Jesus. In His presence you will find the complete, healing water. The Word always points us to the presence of God. God does not mean for us to stop at the reading and inspiration of His Word. He wants it to lead us to experience the Word made flesh by spending "soaking" time in His presence so we walk in the fullness of relationship with Him.

For healing, we must spend time in His presence in progressive intimacy. The angel leads Ezekiel to the water and at the first place where he stops, he steps in the water up to his ankles, then it goes to his knees, then his chest, and finally he is in the water that has gotten so deep he has to swim, he cannot cross anymore unless he lets go and flows with the current. That is the progression of soaking in God's presence as our prayer and study life grow. It allows Him to take over more and more of our heart until we are overflowing in the power of His dynamic, moving presence.

When the angel helps Ezekiel back to the bank, he points out that the destination of this water (the end result) is a place of healing, "for they will be healed, and it shall be that every living thing that moves, wherever the rivers go, will live" (v. 9). Eventually, if you choose to keep moving with this water, you will be healed. This is a unique journey that only you can take with God. The point of these "healing" spas is to get in that water and spend the time soaking in it. God's plan for every believer is total healing and abundant life, but the path to it requires stepping into His water deeper and deeper and going with it—wherever it leads.

The cleansing and healing will lead you to a place of refreshing. Psalm 46:4 explains that this river "shall make glad the city of God." Simply, you will get to the place of refreshing where getting in the water is a pleasure that you long for as much as that warm bath after a long day.

Psalm 46 also talks about the waters of the earth that "roar" and are "troubled." In this world, we can spend a lot of time and energy in troubled waters. Have you ever felt like you live in the midst of that roaring and troubled water and you desperately want God to transport you to the water of His refreshing?

For so long I lived in the roaring and troubled water. I walked in anger and frustration every day. Jim and the kids will tell you that living around me was like "walking on eggshells." You had to do it gently and carefully because I would get angry and blow, and then retreat behind a wall of anger and disappointment which could stay erected for days. One morning my then four-year-old daughter, Heather, came in saying, "Mommy, I know you have to get angry all the time, but ..." I didn't hear anymore after that. It was like someone had slapped me in the face when she said that so matter-of-factly.

At that moment, it was so clear that I lived an angry life and it had to change. I did not want to get angry, but in the next breath I defended my anger as justified because of the stress and pressure in my life. I knew it was wrong and hurting my marriage and kids. I had to deal with it. I read books. I tried so hard in my own strength to control my anger. I cried out to God to take it away.

Why didn't the books and prayers help? Well, they did a little, but you see it was like cutting a weed down without getting rid of the roots. What I needed was healing, deep healing in the recesses of my heart. The roots of my anger were not dealt with until I got serious about getting before the Lord and getting on the altar, laying down all that I thought, expected, and felt owed.

He began to separate my soul and spirit with the cleansing water of His Word, the Holy Spirit guiding me (Heb. 4:12). I began to pray regularly that God would "search me... and know my heart; try me and know my anxieties; and see if there is any wicked way in me, and lead me in the way everlasting," (Psalm 139:23-24 NKJV). I once read that a man decided he would never again say to God anything He did not totally mean and that is when His life really began to change. I began to mean those prayers with all my heart—I was ready to go wherever the river was going to take me. I just wanted to get out of the troubled waters I was so used to swimming in.

What did that do for me? God started to put His finger on the roots of unforgiveness, and selfishness that had to be ripped out before the anger was going to change with any lasting success. While I soaked in the water of God's presence, God took me through inner healing. He would bring incidents and issues into my mind and heart that I needed to deal with. Then as I would give each thought or hurt or ugly piece of my heart to Him, and grieve and release what He showed me, He would pour out grace and healing. It was an exchange—my angry self for His grace and character.

I realized new attitudes come from a new heart. God is the only one who can give you a new heart and mind that has been transformed through His Presence and His Word. As time went on, more and more roots got pulled. I want to strongly encourage you to soak in His waters until you get recharged and healed!

My friend, God knows it takes time to mature and change. First you move in to your ankles, then your knees, then you want more and trust God enough to respond up to your chest. The more you mature, the more you want to empty yourself of your own ways, and the more God can fill you with His. God, the living water, who fills all in all will fill up whatever room you make for Him. He wants to fill you to overflowing.

Ezekiel then sees in verse 12 that there are trees lining the bank on both sides. These trees have leaves that do not wither, and their "fruit will not fail." Psalm 1:3 tells us that those who meditate on God's word are these trees. How can we be those trees? By doing what it says in the verse before. The Message Bible puts it so well: "you thrill to God's word, you chew on scripture day and night. You're a tree replanted in Eden, bearing fresh fruit every month, Never dropping a leaf, always in blossom," (Psalm 1:2). Trees in blossom are beautiful and have vitality. Imagine being always in blossom with leaves that never wither. Many women are afraid of getting old and useless, but that does not happen by the river of God.

What does it mean to meditate or chew on God's word? The Hebrew form of meditation as it refers to in Psalm 1:2 is the word "hagah" (Strong's #1897) which means to reflect, ponder, mutter and moan, contemplating something as one repeats the words. In the Hebrew thought process, meditation was literally repeating the words in a soft, droning sound to yourself. From this comes "davening", a special type of Jewish prayer which involved getting lost in communion with God while you rocked back and forth. Literally, it is praying God's Word, connecting with Him, utterly abandoning any outside distractions, the marriage again of the presence in prayer and the Word, leading us to deep, intimate union with our God. This is the meditation God intended for us to exercise, not the counterfeit we see in other spiritual practices.

I was in a used bookstore in Portland, Oregon and a book caught my eye while mulling around the religion and psychology sections. As I thumbed through it, I realized, the book, How God Changes Your Brain, was about findings that a neuroscientist, Andrew Newberg, made related to the beneficial effects on people physically, mentally and spiritually as you contemplate God and practice spirituality. This was not a Christian book, but it piqued my interest. I wondered what this self-proclaimed agnostic found that he considered "breakthrough findings" after four years of brain-scanning all types of religious people as they meditated on God. Was there any specific type of meditation that was beneficial to slow aging and recharge someone's emotions and memory?

After reading the book, I found there was! What was it? You guessed it! It was the process that curiously resembled davening, the Hebrew form of prayer and meditation referred to in Psalm 1. The benefits, which are well documented in the book, included reducing stress and anxiety, while increasing alertness and brain functioning. The researchers found, though, that a meditator had to practice this for at least fifteen minutes a day and it had to be a regular practice. The longer someone meditates, the more pronounced the benefits are for their stronger brain functioning, slower cell aging, better immunity to disease, increased compassion for others, and better regulation between thoughts and feelings. Wow! It was God's Inside-out Plan! Not bad findings for a book that did not even set out to prove that it was beneficial for us to meditate on God's Word, and back up Psalm 1 with scientific proof!

The angel tells Ezekiel that these trees have fruit that is used for food and leaves for medicine or healing. Just as God heals you, you will go out and heal others. In the Song of Songs, God refers to His bride as the Rose of Sharon. It is so interesting that this was not just a beautiful flower. In Israel it was valued for far more than its looks. The Rose of Sharon can heal others and bring them back to health! God has already prepared works for you to do. As His beautiful rose, you will bring healing and life to others. You are much more to Him than just a pretty face; your value goes much deeper. Let Him fill you with His healing, living water and pour you out.

The angel tells Ezekiel a curious thing in 47:11. He says that the swamps and marshes adjacent to the river will not be healed. The swamps and marshes are stagnant, they do not keep moving forward joining with the river. Some water from the river once gave them life, but they did not keep the water fresh by keeping it flowing in and out. Those swamps and marshes are the areas people get sidetracked in, causing them to stop spending time in God's presence and to stop moving with Him to the final destination. The cares of this world, and other trials and difficulties, can take us down side roads that fill our time and sap our strength, which can eventually cause death. Determine that you will not stop in those places, no matter how strongly the current in life makes you want to settle there.

Get rid of all the marshy distractions that keep you from your time with Him. Empty out your vessel of activities, entertainments, and material things keeping you from doing what you need to do to be with Him. You need to get filled and keep flowing in that healing, refreshing water.

Many women are "filled up" doing good things for God, church, and family, not leaving much room for God's presence to fill them. The enemy loves trapping people in the marshes of busyness so we are not getting the fresh infilling of God's presence each day. I can remember the old saying I learned in church as a kid, "if the devil can't make you bad, he'll make you busy."

Jesus' friends, Mary and Martha, are a great example of how we can fill our time in good distractions. When Jesus came to dinner at their home, although both loved Him and wanted to please Him, they responded to His presence in very different ways. Jesus refused to direct Mary to help prepare the dinner, even when asked by a frustrated and overburdened Martha. Jesus said this was because Mary chose the "one thing" that is "needed"—not desired, or fit in after the activities, but needed. Martha saw what she felt had to be accomplished, but it robbed her of "the good part" of being in relationship with Jesus (Luke 10:38-42). The relationship was what Jesus desired most. He was not as interested in having her prepare a great meal, as He was in spending time with her.

Luke notes that Martha was the one who invited Jesus for dinner! She was the reason Mary even had the opportunity to spend time with Jesus, yet she gets caught up in what she felt had to be accomplished to please Jesus rather than just being with Him. Mary was refreshed and filled by the joy of sitting at God's feet, while Martha was frazzled and annoyed at Mary for not doing what she thought was important to make Jesus happy.

Baptism, His Word, and His Presence are the waters God will use to beautify you. He wants to cleanse, equip, heal, and refresh you in a way that you will never thirst again as you "draw from the wells of salvation," (Isaiah 12:3) becoming a diamond beauty.

Chapter 6
The Fires of Sanctification

Everything we have learned so far is to get to the place where we are ready for God's ultimate beauty treatment: the fires of sanctification. In the last chapter, we talked about how God washes you and cleanses you, but it's in the fire of sanctification that the strength and brilliance of diamond beauty gets fully formed and set in a believer's life. Diamonds are made in the deepest parts of the earth under tremendous pressure and at extremely high temperatures. The heat and pressure turn ordinary dust, known as carbon into the most valuable gem known to man.

Starting at the beginning of human existence, the Lord explained how He created man in Genesis 2:7 NKJV, "And the Lord God formed man of the dust of the ground, and breathed into his nostrils the breath of life; and man became a living being." Then we read in Malachi 3:17 (NKJV) the Lord declares of His people, "And they shall be Mine, says the Lord of hosts, in that day when I publicly recognize and openly declare them to be My jewels (My special possession, My peculiar treasure)." It has been God's plan all along to transform man from that original state of dust to reflect the glory of God and His image, the pinnacle of which is seen in Revelation.

In Revelation 21:9-11 AMP an angel shows the apostle John what Jesus' bride looks like: "Then one of the seven angels... came and spoke to me. He said, Come with me! I will show you the bride, the Lamb's wife. Then in the Spirit he conveyed me away to a vast and lofty mountain and exhibited to me the holy (hallowed, consecrated) city of Jerusalem descending out of heaven from God, clothed in God's glory [in all its splendor and radiance]. The luster of it resembled a rare and most precious jewel, like jasper, shining clear as crystal." Most scholars agree that the jasper John is seeing is a totally pure diamond.

What made the bride radiant was her holiness. In Greek, to "sanctify" (Strong's #37) means to bring into a state of holiness. When we walk through the fires of sanctification (1 Cor. 15:45-49, Romans 8:29) with all its heat and pressure, we form diamond beauty. The same heat and pressure that is naturally applied to make a diamond strong and transparent, God will spiritually apply to you to make you strong, and brilliantly reflect His light as His bride "radiant in holiness." (Ephesians 5:27)

Although holiness can be an obscure concept in our modern world, it is essential to allow God to transform us with this beauty treatment if we want to reflect diamond beauty. If you recall from the earlier chapters, salvation is the restoration process that makes you beautiful from the inside-out. Jesus saved us from our sins to enable us to live a holy life.

In 1Thessalonians 4:7 NKJV Paul exhorts, "For God did not call us to be impure, but to live a holy life." Even though Jesus' sacrifice and death on the cross is what makes us holy by grace, God desires and calls for us to make every effort to live holy as we walk with Him. When I began to understand what holiness really is and why it is God's key process in forming diamond beauty, it became clear why David would ask for God to take him through the fire--so he could be holy: "Examine me, O Lord, and prove me, try (refine by fire) my mind and my heart," (Psalm 26:2 NKJV).

Holiness by Any Other Name

Let's start off by defining the different aspects of holiness—purity, consecration, and sanctification. Each word has a slightly different meaning that, when put together, helps us understand the concept more fully.

Purity means freedom from any kind of contamination, morally or physically. It is something clean and clear. In Old Testament worship, the purer or holier something was, the more perfect or excellent it was, and the ability to be part of it became more exclusive. The godlier and purer you become, the smaller the circle of those that are willing to go with you. I say the word willing because God is willing to take us as far as we want to go. From the beginning of His relationship with Israel, His people, He told them "You shall be holy, for I, the Lord your God am holy," (Lev. 19:2 NKJV). He never calls us to do or be something without giving us the resources or ability to do it. The writer of Hebrews encourages us that we can come "boldly to the throne of grace, that we may obtain mercy and find grace in time of need," (Hebrews 4:16 NKJV) God will always give you what you need to be holy.

As the world moves farther and farther away from obeying biblical principles, we will find ourselves in a smaller circle of those willing to follow God's plans for living "holy." I remember being a college student in the 80's, and it was not unusual for many of the girls to still be virgins into their college years. I became a serious Christian during my junior year and made a commitment to stay pure sexually, but the teasing and criticism I got from others became stronger as I got older. I remember friends telling me that a man would never want to stay in a serious relationship with me if I did not sleep with him before marriage. Now, in my counseling practice, I have middle and high school girls telling me about their sexual experiences and pornography exposure as the normal standard for girls. Typical questions for teens and young adults to get to know each other today are whether they like boys, girls, or both. That was unthinkable for me and my friends in the teen years, and we were typical teens back then.

Today in the mental health field, we are advised to champion and support people struggling with same sex attraction and gender identity issues. In the older DSM manuals, which are the diagnostic guides for the mental health fields, most LGBTQIA+ issues were considered disorders that mental health professionals were supposed to treat. The current prevailing wisdom is that the reasons the depression and suicide rates were so much higher in those populations is because of the stigma and lack of acceptance.

Today when I talk to most young people, they overwhelmingly support this community. Schools are bending over backwards in policies to make sure every student is accepted. If anything is said publicly about the LBGT community that suggests a lack of support, the person saying it is "cancelled" and is considered to be speaking "hate speech," seriously jeopardizing their social standing, safety, and even career. Yet statistics still have not changed. As of 2021, depression rates are still much higher and, according to the CDC, suicide rates in LGBT youth are around 23%, while heterosexual rates are around 6%.[19]

I strongly advise you not to set your standard as what the culture is currently telling you is best. Even though culture shouts that we are being progressive when we embrace these changing moral standards, it admits in the same breath that suicide, depression and anxiety rates are still at all-time highs. Is that really accidental?

God's standards do not change (Hebrews 13:8), and He calls us to be set apart from our culture. God made our bodies as a gift we give to each other when we have a covenant commitment to respect and love each other. The purer and more special we choose to make that gift, the more that gift is valued.

I am happy to report that men actually respect my firm boundary to "save myself for marriage." As I have already told you, the ones that broke up with me after refusing their advances, saved me a lot of heartache from being with someone that did not respect me and was just interested in their own selfish fulfillment. I got married at the ripe old age of twenty-four to a man that was praying for a girl with the convictions I had! Since then, I have met many people who have regretted lowering their standards and not choosing holiness, but I have never met anyone who regretted their commitment to purity in their bodies, minds, or habits.

Purity and consecration go together. When something is consecrated, it means it is separated for God. That could mean people, (Numbers 3:12-13; Numbers 6:8; Leviticus 27:1-8; Exodus 19:6; Exodus 19:10 Exodus 19:14), but it could also mean animals and objects (Exodus 29:37, 30:29; Lev 6:10), and times of the year.

Bible commentator, David Hildebrand, writes that in the Old Testament: "The nearer the relationship to Yahweh who is holy, the greater the separation from imperfection. For example, the Holy of Holies (the inner part of the Jewish temple) is the most separate spot and evidences the highest quality of materials and craftsmanship. The high priest only enters on one day of the year, and with no one else in the next room who might see in (Leviticus 16:17). Spanning out from the sanctuary are concentric circles of decreasing holiness—the Levites, the twelve tribes, the unclean and the heathen (Gentiles)."[20] In other words, the more consecrated, the more separate and perfect something was.

Then there is the word sanctification. Generically, it means, "the state of proper functioning."[21] Something is sanctified when it is being used the way it was designed to be used. When a car is being driven or a ball is being thrown, you could say technically they are sanctified because they are fulfilling the purpose for which they were made. We have been created to function in an optimal way physically, emotionally, and spiritually which God has organized in the way He created the universe. What we eat, our sexuality, even what we watch on TV, or what we read all influence our optimal functioning. When we walk in those things the way God has planned for our benefit, we are living sanctified lives.

When we put purity, consecration, and sanctification together, we realize holiness is being set apart from the rest of the world because we have a special relationship with God. Because of that relationship, we grow into perfection, and become fully functional in the purpose for which we have been made (Ephesians 2:10 NKJV).

The Fire of Affliction

Now that you understand the meaning of holiness, here comes the tough part. The way to holiness is through the fire of hard times and pressure. This is because:

1. Our own actions and responses need to be purified (Malachi 3:3; Psalm 51:6; Isaiah 48:10; Zechariah 13:9) and the ungodly ones "burned off."

2. Our obedience and godliness will lead to suffering for righteousness' sake (Matt 5:11, 12; 1 Peter 1:6-7).

So, you see, there is really no way around it. You are burned if you do, and burned if you don't! But the result of what we become is worth it. In Isaiah 61:3 (AMP) God explains what He gives you for the ashes that are left:

"To grant [consolation and joy] to those who mourn in Zion—to give them an ornament (a garland or diadem) of beauty instead of ashes, the oil of joy instead of mourning, the garment [expressive] of praise instead of a heavy, burdened, and failing spirit—that they may be called oaks of righteousness [lofty, strong, and magnificent, distinguished for uprightness, justice, and right standing with God], the planting of the Lord, that He may be glorified." A result of the fire is the beauty, joy, heart of praise and strength that makes life so fulfilling.

God, Himself, is the one who takes you through the process, the master refiner who knows how to perfect you. Malachi 3:2 says, "For He is like a refiner's fire and like launderers' soap." A refiner takes a piece of silver and puts it over the hottest part of a flame. That is the only way the silver melts enough to have the impurities, known as dross, come to the surface and separate.

He sits there with the piece of silver in his hands the entire time, keeping his eyes on it for every second it is in that fire. If it is left there for only a few seconds too long, it becomes damaged. He will not leave it there any longer than the perfect time for the impurities to be pulled out and then he takes it out immediately. The way a refiner knows that the silver has been purified is when he can see his reflection in it. How much is that like our

God? God watches us every second we are in the fire of affliction, taking us out as soon as His purpose is accomplished and we reflect Him.

One of my fires of affliction was when God allowed us to go through a deep trial concerning our home. We wanted to live closer to the church we were pastoring at the time, and decided we would begin to look for a new house. We found one, but I had an uncomfortable sense in my heart it was not the right fit. Then a woman in the congregation approached us the very Sunday we were planning to sign a contract on the house and said she would drive by this other house every day and pray, feeling we were meant to live in it. She said it was quite large, but vacant.

We decided to drive by it out of curiosity. It was a beautiful brick mansion, but it was not finished inside. It would still require a lot of work and seemed to be out of reach for us financially. But we were looking for a "sign" from God and the apparent confirmation was that I had found this exact house in a magazine several years earlier and had saved it as the perfect house for our family. Since the timing was uncanny, it was a house design we loved, and it had many details on the property we had talked about putting in our next house, we rationalized that this must be God.

We took a step, justifying our decision with many scriptures we felt supported our desire, and bought it. We did it impulsively and without the means to do the finished work needed, calling that faith. We prayed through the whole three years we owned the house as our finances ran dry and we toiled and sweated "in faith" to accomplish what we felt, because of our own desires, was God's will.

He allowed us to walk through that fiery trial, on our knees every day, dealing with discouragement and having one covetous piece of our hearts come to the surface at a time. Finally at the end, after an extended fast, we realized it was time to let it go and sell it. We finally felt released, and that it would not be a lack of faith not to keep going. We had put all of our time, energy, and resources into trying to accomplish what we wanted God to bless.

That trial burned off pride and lust, but it was very humbling. Now, both Jim and I are much more careful, waiting on Him rather than running ahead trying to get Him to bless what we want to do. The price of pride is a fall, but the result, if we fall the right way, is humility which brings a teachable spirit. That house lesson also taught us the difference between doing things in faith and doing things in presumption. They can look very similar on the outside, but faith has a trust and rest in God, letting Him lead to accomplish the vision, while presumption is working it out in our own strength and self-effort, attaching God's name to it.

Although there were many moments when I did not think I would make it through the financial pressure and strain of building a house that ended in failure and loss, God held me until just the right moment and then it was suddenly over. He will not let you go through fiery trials a moment longer than you can handle. He will carefully watch until the impurities are burned off so you can be made complete and reflect Him. (James 1:3-4)

Another tough thing about fire is that it hurts. Anyone who has ever been burned can attest to that. Once someone goes through that kind of pain, they are very afraid of being too near a flame or the possibility of ever getting burned again. They want to steer clear because they now have an understanding of the reality of the consequences. Hell is eternal fire. God wants you to hate sin as much as He does. He wants you to fear going there.

Did you know that the fear of the Lord is His treasure? In Isaiah 33:6 NKJV it says, "Wisdom and knowledge will be the stability of your times, And the strength of salvation; The fear of the Lord is His treasure." Since the fear of the Lord is the beginning of wisdom (Proverbs 1:7), and wisdom is the way that the greatest blessings of life come (Proverbs 3:13-18), God is giving you a precious gift when he puts fear of Him into your heart. One way that fear comes is through the furnace of affliction as God's discipline to purify you. All the suffering God allows is based on His love for you (Proverbs 3:11) to bless you abundantly as you become a wiser, godlier, humbler version of yourself.

The fire and pressure the diamond endures makes it "adamas." That is the root word of diamond in Greek and means indestructible and unconquerable. God takes you through refining because it will make you and your works strong enough to resist anything that could hurt you. Once you go through the fire and there are only ashes and all impurity is burned off, you are dead and there is nothing left of the old you. Sin has no power over you. Paul says, "For he that has died is free from sin," (Romans 6:7 NKJV). Isaiah 54:17 NKJV says once you have passed through the furnace of affliction, you will be unconquerable. "No weapon formed against you shall prosper, and every tongue which rises against you in judgment, you shall condemn. This is the heritage of the servants of the Lord, and their righteousness is from Me," says the Lord.

All the things you do out of your purified heart will have eternal value, too. 1 Corinthians 3:13 says all works that we do will be tested by fire so that what kind they are will be revealed, and what is pure (done out of obedience) will remain and not get destroyed. God will reward you for those works in heaven which means that those rewards will last forever. The value of holiness never ends but will follow you into eternity.

Suffering for Righteousness' Sake

What about the fire we go through when there is no fault of our own? What about when we have just tried to obey God and we end up in a horrible place? Why would a loving God allow that? Those are the times right before God will bless you abundantly. Those are the fires that lead us to great promotion and the joy of being God's instrument for some of the greatest miracles ever—if we will hang tough and choose to keep trusting God.

In the book of Daniel Shadrach, Meshach, and Abednego literally got thrown into the fire because they continued to honor God before men. Even when the king gave them a chance to compromise, threatening to burn them alive, their response was, "O Nebuchadnezzar, we have no need to answer you in this matter. If that is the case, our God whom we serve is able to deliver us from the burning fiery furnace, and He will deliver us from your hand, O king. But if not, let it be known to you, O king, that we do not serve your gods, nor will we worship the gold image which you have set up," (Daniel 3:16-18 NKJV).

They were determined to walk in holiness and were okay with whatever God chose to do. That kind of obedience and trust allows God to have a free hand to demonstrate His glory and power. The fire that was so hot it burned even the men who threw them in, had no power to hurt them. When they came out of the fire, they did not even smell like smoke (Daniel 3:22, 27). That led to God being glorified by the king and throughout the kingdom, and to their promotion in the government of Babylon (Daniel 3:28-30).

When the fire is the result of suffering at the hands of others, God will be right there with us through every moment. The king looked into the furnace (Daniel 3:24-27) and realized that there were four men standing in the fire "and the form of the fourth is like the Son of God."

CHAPTER SIX

Through the prophet Isaiah, God promises "When you walk through the fire, you shall not be burned, nor shall the flames scorch you, for I am the Lord Your God, The Holy One of Israel, your Savior ...Fear not for I am with you," (Isaiah 43:2b-5a NKJV). I wonder if the Hebrew boys were familiar with those words and thinking of those promises when they were being thrown into Nebuchadnezzar's fire?

One of the most memorable sermons in church was when we had a guest speaker from the Middle East that told us about a time when he was being beaten for being a Christian. While he was on the ground being pummeled by a group of angry men, he said that as he cried out to the Lord, he immediately felt His grace. Then it was as if a blanket came down from heaven and covered him. Amazingly, while he lay there, he did not feel the pain of the blows while the men beat him. After they left, he got up and went his way. God will be with us today, just as he was with Daniel's friends in the furnace.

I am not sure what the heat and pressure of God's refining process will be for your life. For Abraham it was believing for a baby when they were too old to have one; for King David it was running for his life for years as King Saul tried to kill him; for Joseph, it was years in prison; for

Hannah, it was tearfully praying and believing for a baby until Samuel was born; for Mary, it was a seemingly illegitimate pregnancy as an engaged young woman whose fiancé was going to banish her until God intervened. The list goes on and on with men and women who trusted and loved their God, willing to be obedient, regardless of the outcome. The same is true for you. After God applies the fires of sanctification to your life, your reward will be to become God's indestructible diamond, shining with His glory. The holiness that the heat and pressure will bring will make you so pure, you can reflect God brilliantly to the world, a diamond with amazing clarity and great value.

Note: Further Study on Holiness

Why Holiness?

There are several reasons why God wants to make us holy:

1) Optimal Functioning

As we just said, God wants us to be holy so that we are fully functioning in the purpose and unique design He has for us. That includes living in a way that promotes optimal mental and physical health.

Research shows that the Israelites were healthier, stronger and enjoyed a significantly higher quality of life than other people groups, historically. God had very specific dietary, sanitation and moral laws that were very separate from other nations. That spared them from the same pain that other nations who lived in "unholy" ways went through. The same is true of us today. If as God's people, we commit ourselves to holiness, morally and in our personal habits, we will not be as affected by many of the diseases that afflict society as a whole. Just one example is STIs. The transmission of STIs could be virtually eliminated in one generation if people would abstain from perversion or sexual involvement outside of marriage. With no expenditure of money for research or public health programs, but simply by holy living, STIs would eventually be a thing of the past in our world.

Many of the dietary requirements God had for the Israelites were for optimal physical health. A great modern day example of this is Jordan Rubin, a man diagnosed with Crohn's disease as he began college. In his book, *The Maker's Diet*, he chronicles how he recovered from death's door by following a biblical diet. None of the modern medical methods and medicines helped, but God's way worked. He has since become a doctor and nutritionist who has been able to help countless other people get healthy by applying what God told the Israelites centuries ago.

God wants you to enjoy optimal functioning in the work he has called you to do as well. When Jesus was about to ascend back to heaven after his resurrection, He promised that the Holy Spirit would come and empower the disciples and guide them to fulfill their purpose so that all would come to know Him and be saved (Acts 1:8). It is the Holy Spirit's job to guide us into all the truth that God has to reveal to us (John 16:13-15). That guidance includes the specific plans God has for our lives (Jeremiah 29:11). When we sin, not only is the Holy Spirit grieved (Ephesians 4:30), but when we do not follow the Holy Spirit's guidance, it also hampers our ability to function in our purpose and the works God has prepared for us. We either will not know what those works are because we aren't listening, or we won't be ready for them because we have not been living right. To be ready for these good works, Paul explains that we must cleanse ourselves and be "a vessel for honor, sanctified and useful for the Master, prepared for every good work" (2 Timothy 2:21 NKJV).

Optimal functioning and beauty go together. When we are fully functioning in what we were created to do, we can't help but have a spark and satisfaction that will result in making us beautiful.

2) We are to Reflect God to the World

The second reason God wants us to live in a state of holiness is that He wants us to reflect Him to the world. Why? Two reasons:

First, as your father, He wants you to be like Him. We were created in His image (Genesis 2:27) and His plan for every person is to become holy because He is holy (Exodus 19:6; Exodus 15:11; Lev 11:44).

Second, since God's beauty plan is for us to reflect His glory, we have to let His light shine through us. One of the qualities of a diamond is its clarity. The ideal diamond is free from internal flaws and inclusions (particles of foreign material within the stone). These detract from the appearance of the stone and interfere with the passage of light through the stone.[22] The purer the clarity of the diamond, the better it lets the light shine through, and the more precious it is. He wants you to be so pure you are completely transparent so that everyone that sees you, sees His glory.

Paul encourages us to "become blameless and harmless, children of God without fault in the midst of a crooked and perverse generation, among whom you shine as lights in the world," (Philippians 2:15 NKJV). The Amplified Bible calls the lights in this passage stars or beacons. The ancient Greeks believed that diamonds were the splinters of stars that had fallen to the earth.[23] As your dad, God wants you to be a shining star in this world.

3) Holiness Produces Joy

Reason number three for living in holiness is that the source of all joy is God's presence. God inhabits the praises of His people, and calls us to worship Him "in the beauty of holiness." (Psalm 29:2; Psalm 96:9).

When we walk in obedience which is the path of holiness, the result will be joy. Jerry Bridges in The Pursuit of Holiness explains it this way:

"Jesus said, "If you obey my commands, you will remain in my love, just as I have obeyed my Father's commands and remain in His love. I have told you this so that my joy may be in you and that your joy may be complete," (John 15:10-11 NKJV). In this statement Jesus links obedience and joy in a cause-and-effect manner; that is, joy results from obedience. Only those who are obedient—who are pursuing holiness as a way of life—will know the joy that comes from God...The daily experience of Christ's love is linked to our obedience to Him. It is not that his love is conditioned on our obedience. That would be legalism. But our experience of His love is dependent on our obedience." (pg.131-132)[24]

God will love you no matter what, but staying and living in His presence is the experience that makes our lives joyful.

Chapter 7
The Optimal Diet

Is there some magic combination of foods that we can eat that will transport us to that perfect weight or shape? I know that there are many new fads and "diet winds" that blow through the church and world, but none seem to have a lasting effect. Ladies, this area is just like every other one when it comes to possessing diamond beauty. We can focus on the outside, but it must start from our spirit and work out to our bodies for diamond beauty. In this chapter, we will focus on the spiritual food that will cause

lasting beauty. In Ezekiel 16:13, part of the blessing of being God's bride and a part of what made the bride so beautiful was that God fed her with the "pastry of fine flour, wheat and oil." He wants to feed your spirit with the "good things" (Psalm 103:5; Psalm 34:10) that will renew and strengthen you in every way—spirit, soul and body.

Spiritually speaking, before you can begin to "eat" the good things God has prepared for you, you have to be willing to go to His table. In Psalm 23:5 David says God prepares a table and that it is set in the "presence" of your enemies. There are several parts of this that are significant for us. First, in the context of Psalm 23, David is expressing how God meets all his needs and gives him rest even in the most difficult times. It is easy to eat well spiritually, emotionally, and physically when we are at peace and feeling strong, but God sets the table in the middle of our battles when our enemies are right there staring us in the face. He wants to help you in the presence of your enemies—the times when life is tough and you want to give up and drink that bottle of vodka, or eat the entire pan of brownies, or abandon the good spiritual food you got at church and never go back because the relationships are difficult, or when you have had enough of your husband and kids and it is just too hard. God knows you need to come to the table and be fed and strengthened with the "food" He has prepared at that time, and He is ready. The table is prepared and waiting for you.

Psalm 34:8 NKJV bids us, "Oh, taste (ta'am Strong's #2938) and see that the Lord is good." The Hebrew word ta'am involves sampling what is offered and having wisdom to choose the good things. My youngest daughter was very picky and spent 18 years refusing to eat most foods—especially her vegetables. Her pediatrician has told her over (and over) she can develop a taste for something if she eats it several times, even things that she might not initially enjoy. We must develop a hunger and thirst for the things of God to get blessed and filled. David says, "As the deer pants for the water brooks, so pants my soul for You, O God." (Psalm 42:1 NKJV).

The diet transformation starts with choosing to sit down with Him before the daily battle with the enemies you fight all day long, and developing a taste for what He has prepared for you. The thing about the kingdom is that God's ways are the opposite of our natural ways (Isaiah 55:8-11). Our thinking is that we will get full and not be hungry anymore. God's ways are that the more we eat spiritually, the hungrier we get for the things God feeds us. And God will feed us to the fullest every time. The griffon vulture we looked at a few chapters back eats a huge amount of food every time. They eat and eat until they are so full, they can barely take off in flight again. Then they can go for hours without being weary.

The Food on God's Table

You are what you eat. So, what is on the table God sets in the presence of our enemies that will strengthen and nurture us to grow into strong, healthy diamond beauty? I want to focus on the food mentioned in Ezekiel 16 since that chapter describes how God made Israel "exceedingly beautiful" (Ezekial 16:13 AMP). As part of the way He abundantly blessed her, the Lord fed His bride, Israel, "pastry of fine flour, honey and oil." God wants to bless us with abundant life, and His "food" is like pastry—it's rich and satisfying, and as we eat, we will hunger for more.

Bread

Fine flour goes into the making of bread. It is interesting that the largest portion of our natural diet should be devoted to carbohydrates—about 55% according to my fitness app. "Good" carbs are the source of life and vitality. They are the fuel that gives you physical energy and mental clarity, making it possible for you to be strong and productive. Jesus is the bread of life for us—the perfect carb, the ultimate whole grain, making strength and productivity possible to the highest degree.

The tastiest bread is freshly baked. For that kind of quality bread, we must get it and eat it daily. That is the pattern that God instituted for Israel in the wilderness, establishing a daily dependence to get nourishment for His people: "Then the LORD said to Moses, "I will rain down bread from heaven for you. The people are to go out each day and gather enough for that day. In this way I will test them and see whether they will follow my instructions," (Exodus 16:4 NKJV). In the New Testament, when He taught the disciples how to pray, Jesus said to ask for "our daily bread." That prayer can be asked on many levels from literal provision of food to spiritual filling of Jesus into our minds and hearts.

Jesus is the fulfillment of the daily, fresh bread God gave to feed and strengthen His people forever. In the gospel of John 6:53-58 NKJV Jesus said:

> "Most assuredly, I say to you, unless you eat the flesh of the Son of Man and drink His blood, you have no life in you. Whoever eats My flesh and drinks My blood has eternal life, and I will raise him up at the last day. For My flesh is food indeed, and My blood is drink indeed. He who eats My flesh and drinks My blood

> abides in Me, and I in him. As the living Father sent Me, and I live because of the Father, so he who feeds on Me will live because of Me. This is the bread which came down from heaven—not as your fathers ate the manna, and are dead. He who eats this bread will live forever."

After that statement many of His disciples left because they did not understand what He was saying. Jesus was inviting them to dine with Him daily by taking in His life through communion and embracing His sacrifice on the cross. Jesus meant they would have His glorious life within them, providing enough energy and strength to change the world (Acts 1:8; John 6:63).

In Songs of Songs 1:2, the Shulamite, a symbol of us as the Bride of Christ, tells her Beloved, "For your love is better than wine." Christ's love is expressed in the wine of His blood poured out for us at the cross so we can have full fellowship and union with God. The institution of communion brings us to the table individually and corporately to be able to partake in the bread (body) and wine (blood) of our Lord to remember His great act of redemption and to become partakers of his nature through that union with Him (1 Corinthians 5:6-8, 10:1-22, and 11:18-34).

I have had seasons when taking communion daily strengthened me and transformed areas of my life and family. One January, as I prayed about what God wanted me to do to start off the year in the best way, I felt impressed to take communion every morning. I did it every day for the whole month; many days taking it in proxy for my family also. Not only did my fellowship with God in prayer noticeably deepen, but during the next year two of my children that I had been praying for, for seven straight years, recommitted their lives to God for good, and one was dramatically delivered from addiction. I am convinced that taking communion each day was one of the factors that shifted these things.

I have also experienced healing because of people taking communion for me. I was supposed to be in a good friend's wedding who is like a daughter to me. A month before the wedding, I got COVID and it hit me hard. I ended up hospitalized and the fatigue and nausea from the treatment they gave me was crippling, even after I came home. It was about ten days before the wedding and I thought, "there is no way I can have the stamina to even attend, much less to participate as a bride's maid." My friend was devastated and she decided to go to war for me. She fasted, prayed, and took communion on my behalf. I woke up a few days later, and had energy that I had not felt since the onset of the virus. I participated in the wedding and people commented on how well I seemed to be doing. Although still a little tired, I knew that her warfare on my behalf was the difference.

Honey

The International Standard Bible Encyclopedia sums up the significance of honey in ancient Israel:

"A land flowing with milk and honey" suggested a land filled with an abundance of good things (Exodus 3:8,17; Leviticus 20:24; Numbers 13:27; Deuteronomy 6:3; Joshua 5:6; Jeremiah 11:5; Ezekiel 20:6,15). "A land of olive trees and honey" had the same meaning (Deuteronomy 8:8; 2 Kings 18:32), and similarly "streams of honey and butter" (Job 20:17). Honey was a standard of sweetness (Song of Solomon 4:11; Ezekiel 3:3; Revelation 10:9,10). It typified sumptuous fare (Song of Solomon 5:1; Isaiah 7:15,22; Ezekiel 16:13,19). The ordinances of Yahweh were "sweeter than honey and the droppings of the honeycomb" (Psalms 19:10; 119:103). "Thou didst eat .... honey" (Ezekiel 16:13) expressed Yahweh's goodness to Jerusalem."[25]

Honey was a symbol of God's sweetest provision and blessing. My sweet tooth has been handed down from my grandma to my dad to me. It is so strong in me that before the fruit of self-control began to mature in my life, I could and would eat a piece of cheesecake for breakfast—and lunch and dinner—and maybe a small piece for a snack in between. The same would happen with cookies or any kind of pie. Some of you reading this are smiling—you get it. If I could live on apple turnovers, cheesecake, cupcakes and chocolate and it would be good for me, I would be in heaven. That is why I love that God says He fed Israel pastry. That really got my attention. Could God be that good when He takes care of us? The answer is yes a thousand times over—but He has a higher plan than literal sweets. His honey is the Word.

David writes, "How sweet are Your words to my taste, sweeter than honey to my mouth!" (Psalm 119:103 NKJV). And in Psalm 19:10 in the Amplified version he says, "More to be desired are they than gold, even than much fine gold; they are sweeter also than honey and drippings from the honeycomb." Why is the Word and the fear of Him such a blessing that we should desire it even more than gold? Why is it so good that he compares it to honey—the sweetest delicacy of the time? The answer is found in the preceding verses of the same Psalm. Let me explain the meaning of the key words to help you comprehend the depth of how God's Word affects and satisfies us:

- "The law of the Lord is perfect, restoring (rescuing, relieving) the [whole] person
- The testimony of the Lord is sure, making wise (act wisely in mind, word and act) the simple (someone silly, open to be led astray).
- The precepts of the Lord are right, rejoicing (cheering up, making joyful) the heart
- The commandment of the Lord is pure and bright, enlightening (kindling, setting on fire, make shine) the eyes (the appearance, face, look).
- The [reverent] fear of the Lord is clean, enduring forever
- The ordinances of the Lord are true and righteous altogether."

When you understand how "eating" all of God's Word impacts every aspect of who you are, it truly does become more valuable than gold, and sweet as honey.

CHAPTER SEVEN

Oil

The oil that is most referred to in the Bible is olive oil. Olive oil is a fat in our natural diet. Although fats have gotten a bad name, "healthy fats play a huge role in helping you manage your moods, stay on top of your mental game, fight fatigue, and even control your weight."[26] God's table has oil on it for you to dip into liberally that is a wonderful complement to His bread. The oil is the work of His Holy Spirit.

Oil was a staple ingredient in every part of daily life during biblical times. The International Standard Bible Encyclopedia explains two uses of oil:

- As a commodity: "Olive oil when properly made and stored will keep sweet for years, hence, was a good form of merchandise to hold. Oil is still sometimes given in payment (1 Kings 5:11; Ezekiel 27:17; Hosea 12:1; Luke 16:6; Revelation 18:13)."[27]
- As a light: "Olive oil until recent years was universally used for lighting purposes. In Palestine are many homes where a most primitive form of lamp similar to those employed by the Israelites is still in use. The prejudice in favor of the exclusive use of olive oil for lighting holy places is disappearing. Formerly any other illuminant was

forbidden (compare Exodus 25:6; 27:20; 35:8,14,28; 39:37; Matthew 25:3,4,8)."[28]

As I read this, I couldn't help but smile as I thought of Proverbs 31:18 AMP which says, "She tastes and sees that her gain from work [with and for God] is good; her lamp goes not out, but it burns on continually through the night [of trouble, privation, or sorrow, warning away fear, doubt, and distrust]." The NKJ version of that verse says that she perceives "her merchandise" as good. A woman of diamond beauty saturates her heart with the oil of God's Holy Spirit which enables her to look with satisfaction at her "merchandise"—her efforts and accomplishments for God—and know they are valuable and good. Her lamp does not go out because the Spirit is always with her, giving her the strength to handle whatever comes her way. He also is the light of hope in her heart in the darkest of times when she needs the mood stabilizer, fatigue fighter and mind strengthener that God's oil, the Holy Spirit, provides.

Here is a list of how the oil of the Holy Spirit affects all aspects of our lives today just as in Israel's day, which will whet your appetite to get your fresh daily fill:

- He fills us with "exultant joy and gladness" (Our holy mood stabilizer)

"You have loved righteousness and hated lawlessness; Therefore God, Your God, has anointed You with the oil of gladness more than Your companions," (Hebrews 1:9 NKJV).

"To console those who mourn in Zion, To give them beauty for ashes, The oil of joy for mourning," (Isaiah 61 NKJV).

- He fills us with power to fulfill our call and purpose:

"Then Samuel took the horn of oil and anointed him in the midst of his brothers; and the Spirit of the Lord came upon David from that day forward," (1 Samuel 16: 13 NKJV).

- He gives us hope:

"Now may the God of hope fill you with all joy and peace in believing, that you may abound in hope by the power of the Holy Spirit," (Romans 15:13 NKJV).

- He makes us holy:

"He poured some of the anointing oil on Aaron's head and anointed him to consecrate him," (Leviticus 8:12 NKJV).

"that I might be a minister of Jesus Christ to the Gentiles, ministering the gospel of God, that the offering of the Gentiles might be acceptable, sanctified by the Holy Spirit," (Romans 15:16 NKJV).

- He is part of the healing process:

"Is any one of you sick? He should call the elders of the church to pray over him and anoint him with oil in the name of the Lord," (James 5:14 NKJV).

"They drove out many demons and anointed many sick people with oil and healed them," (Mark 6:13).

Foods to Avoid

Just as the Lord has good food for us to eat, the devil is trying to tempt you to feed on the "bad carbs" that will destroy your health and rob you of diamond beauty. Proverbs 31:27 AMP says, "She looks well to how things go in her household, and the bread of idleness (gossip, discontent, and self-pity) she will not eat."

The enemy hopes you will be a carnal Christian that regularly gives in to your enemies and chooses to eat the bread of idleness. The devil knows it tastes sweet at first bite as you indulge your natural desires, but in your heart, mind and body it is wreaking long term havoc that will dull and muddy your ability to develop into a diamond reflecting the glory of Christ. After the initial energy boost, you will not be able to produce and accomplish the works that God has for you because gossip, discontent and self-pity will poison your mind and heart and then the crash will come, robbing you of the blessing God had planned (Psalm 34:8).

Gossip

James 3:2-12 lays out the importance of our tongue and the power it has to hurt us:

> "For we all stumble in many things. If anyone does not stumble in word, he is a perfect man, able also to bridle the whole body. ...But no man can tame the tongue. It is an unruly evil, full of deadly poison. With it we bless our God and Father, and with it we curse men, who have been made in the similitude of God. Out of the same mouth proceed blessing and cursing. My brethren, these things ought not to be so. Does a spring send forth fresh water and bitter from the same opening? Can a fig tree, my brethren, bear olives, or a grapevine bear figs? Thus no spring yields both salt water and fresh."

The poison that comes from "cursing" your fellowman by your words breeds division and strife (friction, conflict, rivalry) (James 3:14-16). The root of strife is pride according to Proverbs 13:10 "By pride comes nothing but strife...." Gossip often occurs because you are jealous or you want to be included in the group of people you are with who are gossiping. Proverbs 26:20 says, "where there is no talebearer, strife ceases." When you stop gossiping, the strife ends and God's peace can take strife's place.

If no man can tame the tongue, then how do we stop and walk away instead of indulging in gossip which poisons us? Jesus gave us the answer when He said, "out of the abundance of the heart, the mouth speaks." (Matthew 12:34). Your heart attitude is the key.

"...God resists the proud, But gives grace to the humble," (Proverbs 3:34 NKJV).

"Therefore submit to God. Resist the devil and he will flee from you. Draw near to God and He will draw near to you," (James 4:7 NKJV).

When you get serious about stopping gossip from coming out of your mouth, you can ask the Holy Spirit every day to bring conviction whenever you start to gossip. He will be faithful to convict you. Then you have the choice to stop and immediately obey the still small voice that corrects you. If I am headed into a situation where I know I will be tempted to gossip, it helps to commit to obey ahead of time before I run into the problem. God will change you as you repent and humble yourself under His care.

Discontent

A discontented person is dissatisfied and has a restless longing for better things.[29] Eating the bread of discontent is a real breeder of unhappiness and depression. The enemy knows if he can get us looking for more because we are discontent with where we are or what we have or who we are, then he can ensure we will be miserable. One of the biggest sources of discontent in our day is social media. As I scroll through my feed, it can easily turn into comparing my life to other people's and it is never a good thing. Paul tells us he handled comparison how in 2 Corinthians 10:12 NKJV, giving us a good model to follow: "For we dare not class ourselves or compare ourselves with those who commend themselves. But they, measuring themselves by themselves, and comparing themselves among themselves are not wise."

People who compare themselves among themselves are not wise. It's a waste of time because God made you to be different and unique. Looking like them or having what they have would never satisfy you because it's not what you were created for.

The writer of Hebrews advised, "Be content with such things as you have. For He Himself has said, 'I will never leave you nor forsake you.'" (Hebrews 13:5 NKJV). King David said, "Whom have I in heaven but You, and there is none upon earth I desire besides you....God is the strength of my heart and my portion forever." (Psalm 73:25 NKJV). God is our portion, our inheritance. David concludes in Psalm 16:5 NKJV, "O Lord, you are the portion of my inheritance and my cup; You maintain (uphold) my lot, the lines have fallen to me in pleasant places; Yes, I have a good inheritance." God gives us what we have and He Himself is our portion. Going to His table so He who "fills all in all" (Ephesians 1:23) can fill you with all the fullness of God (Ephesians 3:19) is the answer to our discontent.

When we focus on what we do not have, we are telling God He has short-changed us and He is not a good provider. We are saying He is not who He says and He has not or is not fulfilling His promises. Sometimes our circumstances might legitimately feel that way. So what do we do? We activate our faith. Our faith substantiates what we do not see at the moment (Hebrews 11:1). Our faith gives us hope because we know God is who He says He is. God cannot NOT be faithful just as you cannot change your DNA. Faithfulness is in His DNA (Hebrews

10:23). If you cannot see how this is true in your situation, do not fret. Wait patiently on Him and you will see it from His perspective (Psalm 37:7-9). Faith comes by hearing the Word of God (Romans 10:17). We need to eat, dining with the Lord in the presence of our enemy, Discontent.

Self-Pity

If misery loves company then discontent's company is often self-pity. They hang out together and feed off of each other. Self-pity is to "pity oneself; especially exaggerated or self-indulgent pity where you believe that you are the victim who has done no wrong and is deserving of condolence from everyone."[30] I want to make clear that I am not speaking of when you have legitimate pain or grief at a difficult time in life. The problem is more of a continual state of "poor me" when you feel sorry for yourself because life is particularly hard for you in your own eyes as compared to others.

Anytime self-pity is being indulged, misery abounds. I used to eat a lot of self-pity. It was my own emotional cheesecake. If my husband was not doing what I wanted—self-pity; if my kids did not respond the way I wanted—self-pity; if work or church was stressful for me—self-pity. Notice how "I" and "me" are the principal players in self-pity. It is selfishness at its most pathetic and annoying. When I considered why I felt sorry for myself, I always came to the realization that my own desires were not being fulfilled in the way I wanted them to be fulfilled. That is the opposite of God's plan in which we die and Christ lives in us to fulfill God's desires (Galatians 2:20, John 4:34).

The worst thing about eating self-pity, aside from the misery, is that it keeps you stuck and powerless. Feeling sorry for yourself because you are a victim makes it impossible to change because blaming people, circumstances or God for your unhappiness means they have to change to make you happy. It gives them all the power. God came to empower you (Ephesians 1:18-20) so you could "be strong in the Lord and in the power of His might," (Ephesians 6:10 NKJV). When we eat self-pity, we disempower ourselves, rejecting the power God could work through us if we handed our desires over to Him, and died to ourselves.

One of a woman's biggest enemies is self-pity, and the enemy places it right by the Lord's table, hoping you will choose to take big helpings of it every day rather than the good carbs God has planned for you.

What do you say we follow the Proverbs 31 woman's lead and refuse to eat the bread of idleness? If you are struggling with any of these "bad carbs," stop and get to

God's table to get filled up with His food. Join with saints through the ages who sat for a while and enjoyed the bread, oil, and honey God has prepared to refresh and strengthen. Thomas a Kempis (1380-1471), the author of *The Imitation of Christ*, prayed, "Turn all earthly things to bitterness for me, all grievances and adversity to patience, all lowly creation to contempt and oblivion...From this moment to all eternity do You alone grow sweet to me, for You alone are my food and drink, my love and my joy, my sweetness and my total good. Let your presence wholly inflame me, consume and transform me into Yourself, that I may become one spirit with You by the grace of inward union and by the melting power of your ardent love."[31]

Note: Additional Food for Thought and Growth

Two other foods that the Bible often references are milk and meat. Here are some notes on these important foods at God's table:

God's invitation to abundant life by feeding on what He has prepared is beautifully expressed in Isaiah 55:1-2:

> "Ho! Everyone who thirsts, come to the waters; And you who have no money, come, buy and eat. Yes,

> come, buy wine and milk without money and without price. Why do you spend money for what is not bread, and your wages for what does not satisfy? Listen carefully to Me, and eat what is good, and let your soul delight itself in abundance."

Isaiah 25:6 (NIV) says at the wedding feast of the Lord and His bride, "the Lord Almighty will prepare a feast of rich food for all peoples, a banquet of aged wine— the best of meats and the finest of wines."

God's table is also set with milk and meat. These are the complete spiritual proteins you need to eat all through your life. In our natural diet proteins are needed to grow and to repair and replace worn out or damaged tissue. A complete protein contains an adequate amount of all the essential amino acids that should be incorporated into a diet. To be considered complete, a complete protein must not lack even one essential amino acid.[32] Milk and meat are complete proteins because they contain all you need to equip you to be a complete, beautiful woman of God (2Tim 3:17). Peter exhorts us, "like newborn babies, crave pure spiritual milk (of the Word), so that by it you may grow up in your salvation," (1Peter 2:2 NIV). Paul tells us, we need to mature so we "will no longer be infants, tossed back and forth by the waves, and blown here and there by every wind of teaching and by the cunning and craftiness of people in their deceitful scheming." (Ephesians 4:14 NIV) God nourishes us for growth when we are baby Christians through the milk of the Word. Milk is a complete meal and breast milk is specially formulated to contain all the amino acids a baby needs for optimal growth which occurs most quickly during the first years of life. God knows your primary growth and learning years are at the beginning of your spiritual life. That is when you learn to walk without tottering and falling, securely learning and knowing the doctrines of the Word (Hebrews 6:1-2), and you learn to talk, in edification and godliness (James 3:2). Milk is easily digested, and it builds up.

Then as we grow, God begins to set the table with meat. Meat is the solid food that is beyond a baby's ability to process and handle. In Hebrews 5:13-14 AMP the writer explains the difference between a milk and meat eater:

> "For everyone who continues to feed on milk is obviously inexperienced and unskilled in the doctrine of righteousness (of conformity to the divine will in

purpose, thought, and action), for he is a mere infant [not able to talk yet]! But solid food is for full-grown men, for those whose senses and mental faculties are trained by practice to discriminate and distinguish between what is morally good and noble and what is evil and contrary either to divine or human law."

Mature Christians are the ones who are skilled and experienced in conforming to God's will in their purpose, thought, and action. They are the ones who no longer are filled with their own ways (1 Corinthians 3:1-3) with life revolving around their own needs as a baby's does. They are the ones who say, "My food is to do the will of Him who sent Me, and to finish His work," (John 4:34 NKJV). They are the ones for whom the basics of repentance from dead works and faith and baptism and the laying on of hands and the resurrection of the dead and eternal judgment have been digested and understood as the "basics" of Christianity (Hebrews 6:1-2). They are the ones who have hungered and thirsted for righteousness and whom God has completely satisfied (Matthew 5:6; Isaiah 55:1-3).

So, to answer the question of whether God has a diet for us, I would say yes! God's spiritual diet of pastry, honey, oil, wine, and meat is designed to fill us up to the fullest and make us the healthiest version of ourselves spiritually, where true health starts. Because God's ways aren't our ways, the more we eat, the hungrier we will get, and the more He will feed us (without gaining a physical ounce). He has a limitless supply of food to strengthen you and help you grow in all the things He has promised for your life. The only thing you need to do to receive this fabulous meal is come to the table.

Chapter 8
A Royal Wardrobe

The clothes we wear say a lot about us. When I was in high school, you could identify the group a person belonged to just by what they wore. A "preppy" wore certain designer labels and colors—usually there was a lot of navy and pink going on. A "jock" wore letter jackets and athletic gear. As a therapist, when I worked with teens in the inner city, some of them would talk about gang "colors"; if you wore those colors it meant you were part of a certain gang and everyone knew it.

God also has spiritual clothes He has prepared for you from the time you become His so everyone knows you belong to Him. In fact, God has an outfit prepared for you as soon as you repent and give your heart to Him. When the prodigal son decided to return to His father's house, the father came running to him and the first thing He did was tell the servants, "Bring quickly the best robe (the festive robe of honor) and put it on him; and give him a ring for his hand and sandals for his feet," (Luke 15:22 NKJV). The servants stripped off the old filthy rags he was wearing and dressed him in the clothes of a son and honored person. God has a royal wardrobe for you because of the value you have to Him as His own. Once you become His, you exchange your own standards of righteousness, which the Bible says are like rags (Isaiah 64:6), and put on God's "robe of righteousness" (Isaiah 61:10).

God wants you to know you are both a princess and a priestess, and He clothes you accordingly. You do not have to earn or pay for it. In Ezekiel 16:10-12 NKJV, the Lord explains to Israel: "I clothed you with an embroidered dress and put sandals of fine leather on you. I dressed you in fine linen and covered you with costly garments. I adorned you with jewelry: I put bracelets on your arms and a necklace around your neck, and I put a ring on your nose, earrings on your ears and a beautiful crown on your head."

He chooses to give you this costly clothing that you could never buy on your own. It cost Jesus, the only one who could pay the price for it, His life. That is why it is such an honor to wear it. God chooses us and clothes us with all that salvation means (Psalm 103:1-5)— forgiveness, healing, eternal life, God's lovingkindness and mercy, and all the good things He feeds us to renew us and restore us to abundant life (John 10:10).

The realization of the significance of the garments of salvation, which can only be worn by the saints of God, evokes a response of joy and gratefulness:

Psalm 30:11 NKJV, "You have turned for me my mourning into dancing; You have put off my sackcloth and clothed me with gladness"

Psalm 132:16 NKJV, "I will also clothe her priests with salvation, And her saints shall shout aloud for joy.

The specific garments God adorns us with to reflect His glory as stated in Ezekiel 16:10-12 are dresses (coverings) made of linen, sandals of fine leather, and a jewel crowned headdress. Let's see what they mean for us and why they will make us "shout aloud for joy."

Dresses of Linen

Linen is mentioned as an important fabric from the beginning of the establishment of the nation of Israel in Exodus to the marriage feast of Jesus in the last book of the Bible, Revelation. The curtains of the tabernacle, God's dwelling, and the veil that was in front of His presence were all made of linen (Exodus 26:1, 31) The priests were dressed in it (Exodus 28:4-8; Lev. 6:10). The Proverbs 31 woman, a composite of the perfect woman, is clothed in it: "Her clothing is of linen, pure and fine, and of purple [such as that of which the clothing of the priests and the hallowed cloths of the temple were made]" (Proverbs 31:22 AMP). And the bride is dressed in it for the marriage feast as described in Revelation 19:8 NKJV, "And to her it was granted to be arrayed in fine linen, clean and bright, for the fine linen is the righteous acts of the saints."

The characteristics of linen give us understanding about why God chooses for us to be "arrayed" in it. It is an honor because it parallels the process of sanctification we go through as His beloved children and represents the value He has for us. In ancient cultures, because of the labor intensive and difficult process to make linen, it was reserved only for royalty. Once you become a Christian, Peter explains "you are a royal priesthood, a holy nation, His own special people" (1 Peter 2:9 NKJV).

The fibers of flax plants are very strong, but they can be easily damaged during collection and must be handled with great care, just as we must handle our faith with great care. While we are on the way to attaining diamond beauty, we must be careful that we do not get choked out by the daily trials, temptations, and concerns until our faith matures and we become fruitful (Matt 13:3-9). Once the stems have been collected, they must be "retted," or stripped down into their essential fibers. This is done by treating them in water. God strips us down, cleans us up and heals us through the water treatments we apply. Next the fibers have to be combed to separate the soft from the stiff materials, then filtered so that only the soft remain. God as the master craftsman carefully takes us through the process of being transformed until we are strong and ready for use as His prized "poiema." Finished linen has a smooth, flawless appearance. It has a slight shiny quality to it, but is very comfortable and feels very soft (Matt 11:30). God's value for you as His beloved is expressed in the careful care, washing, and sifting He has you go through until you are sanctified, only the gentle parts remain, and you are shining with His glory.

Then Revelation 19:8 gives an understanding of how the world sees us wear this linen covering. The world sees it through how you live and what you do. It sees "the fine linen which is the righteous acts of the saints." Our everyday behavior and decisions based on our obedience, reverence, and trust in our Lord, will allow God's light to shine in and through us. These actions are not some grand gestures of sacrifice. As we walk in these daily acts it makes us strong and secure today just as it did the Proverbs 31 woman. That strength is further explained in Isaiah 30:15 which says, "In quietness and confidence shall be your strength." The quietness (Strong's #8252) Isaiah speaks of is the same quietness of spirit (Strong's #2272) Peter tells women about when he continues to follow up explaining what holy conduct looks like in I Peter 3:4 NKJV, "Do not let your adornment be merely outward—arranging the hair, wearing gold, or putting on fine apparel— rather let it be the hidden person of the heart, with the incorruptible beauty of a gentle and quiet spirit, which is very precious in the sight of God."

In my life, I have seen my husband and family change with much less work on my part as I have developed a gentle and quiet attitude. Proverbs 25:15 NKJV says, "By long forbearance (patience) a ruler is persuaded, and a gentle tongue breaks a bone." When I am humble and patient in my approach during a disagreement with my husband, he is much quicker to consider what I am saying. When I put my confidence in God, He will usually do the work needed in my husband's and my heart or just arrange circumstances to take care of me Himself as he did with Sarah and Abraham.

In her case, Sarah agreed to let Abraham tell people she was his sister because he was afraid they would kill him because of her beauty (Genesis 20). It was technically true that they were related, but it put her in danger of being sexually approached by another man. That was a scary situation for her to be in as a married woman. You would have thought that by this point, after so many encounters with God, Abraham would have had the faith to know God would take care of him no matter what the circumstances were. Abraham wasn't doing his job. He was only thinking of himself rather than the precarious position he was putting her in.

Rather than reaming Abraham out, she quietly submitted and trusted God. God sovereignly told the king of the land, Abimelech, in a dream, that Sarah was Abraham's wife and if he touched her, he would be a dead man (Genesis 20:4). Then Abimelech went to Abraham and reamed him out for what he did. On top of that, he gave Sarah a thousand pieces of silver to take away any damage this situation had done to her honor. God took care of her beyond Abraham's ability and faith.

In my case, I really felt God wanted me to go back to school and get my master's degree as a marriage and family therapist. We had just moved to a place where there was an excellent university less than a mile from my house that happened to have a program in therapy. However, one of our kids had just started college and another would be going the following year. Jim had started a new job in an area that had much higher housing costs than where we had previously lived. Not to mention we had just been through a difficult building situation in which we lost money on a house and were having trouble selling it.

It was the worst time for me to go back from a financial standpoint, but I really felt it was the right thing to do. I kept getting prompted by the Lord to have faith and apply when I prayed. I applied and got accepted. Jim then informed me that if I wanted to go, I would have to finance it without taking a loan out or expecting any money from his salary, because there was no way to work it out within our family's current budget. His exact words were, "If it is God's will for you to do this, then He is going to have to pay for it."

I prayed, put it in God's hands, and then learned about assistantships which covered tuition for classes in exchange for working at the university's graduate office. That would be a stretch for me, because I had no computer office experience, but felt I should apply. If it was God's will for me to go to school, I had to be diligent to look into any opportunities that presented themselves.

A few weeks later, I got a call from the school for an interview for an assistantship that had just opened. They told me if I got the job, it could cover all my tuition, and they would work out a schedule around my classes and around my kid's school schedules. The dean who interviewed me expressed concern that I did not have as much computer experience as the typical applicant, but said they would call with a decision in a few days, after finishing their remaining interviews.

As time went on with no news about the job, I was fearful and anxious, as I knew I had to register and pay for classes by the end of the week. I kept praying, wondering if I had really heard from God about going to school. The phone rang with two days left before registration, but I was not home to take the call. When I got home, my then eight-year-old daughter, Sage, told me she had a funny talk with a lady "named Dean" who wanted me to call her. My heart raced as I called back right away. The dean informed me I had the job, laughing about my charming little daughter who could not understand why a lady would be named Dean.

During the next three years, that assistantship helped me to learn excellent computer skills, paid for every penny of my graduate education, and worked around my kid's school schedules so I did not miss one event or school pick-up. I also realized as the new assistant, who took the 20-30 applications each semester from aspiring applicants for the three assistantships available, how amazing it was that I got this job. The applicants were usually bright young men and women who invariably had much more office and computer training than I started out with and usually were not concerned about schedule constraints because of their kids. Yet God opened the door for me to get the job. "What then shall we say to these things? If God is for us, who can be against us?" (Romans 8:31 NKJV).

It was truly a faith building experience where God sovereignly provided for me beyond Jim's and my own abilities. My "acts" in obedience to God's direction of applying to school, working through the assistantship, and now helping others have dressed me in a way that I have more strength and confidence than at any other time in my life.

The good deeds that come out of your obedience are pleasant and "very precious" in His sight. These acts of love and obedience are the linen "dress" that clothes you with honor and beauty now in front of this world, and in eternity before God as His glorious bride. Proverbs 31:31 (NLT) declares, "Reward her for all she has done. Let her deeds publicly declare her praise."

Sandals of Fine Leather

I have to say here, the fact that God wants to dress you and me in fine leather sandals gives me much personal joy—almost as much as the pastry in the last chapter. There is nothing to lift my mood like a great pair of shoes! All throughout history women have loved great, colorful shoes. After some research on the subject, I discovered wealthy women and heads of state in ancient Eastern cultures would wear purple or red shoes made of fine leather skins. The colors of these shoes signified royalty and importance.

God has a way for us to walk in the shoes He gives us to fill. Isaiah 52:7 says, "How lovely on the mountains are the feet of him who brings good news, who announces peace and brings good news of happiness, who announces salvation, and says to Zion, "Your God reigns!" In Romans 10:15 Paul writes, "How will they preach unless they are sent? Just as it is written: "How beautiful are the feet of those who preach the gospel of peace, who bring glad tidings of good things!" God puts you in those fine shoes so you are the one who can walk into a situation where people need hope and peace.

Wearing God's shoes directs our steps and show us the direction in which we should walk (Psalm 119:105). Walking in the path of the Word brings the experience of walking in daily peace. In John 16:33 Jesus tells His disciples that "These things I have spoken to you, that in Me you may have peace. In the world you will have tribulation; but be of good cheer, I have overcome the world." The Word brings peace.

How do we get our feet shod with this peace in the middle of the crazy daily race of life? We must pursue it:

Romans 14:19 NKJV: "Therefore let us pursue the things which make for peace and the things by which one may edify another."

2 Timothy 2:22 NKJV: "Flee also youthful lusts; but pursue righteousness, faith, love, peace with those who call on the Lord out of a pure heart."

Hebrews 12:14 NKJV: "Pursue peace with all people, and holiness, without which no one will see the Lord."

1 Peter 3:10-11 NKJV quoting Psalm 34:14: "He who would love life and see good days...let him seek peace and pursue it."

That idea of pursuing in these verses goes back to idea of the Hebrew word "radaph" (Strong's #7291) which means to run after or chase. You cannot chase anything without good shoes. God constructs those shoes with His Word being the "leather" that enables you to run after peace and attain it because the Word teaches you how to live in the kingdom (Eph 6:15). "For the kingdom of God is not eating and drinking, but righteousness and peace and joy in the Holy Spirit" (Romans 14:17 NKJV).

The sturdiest shoes of our royal wardrobe, those which will enable us to walk on God's path and protect us from the enemy's lies, are constructed by the Word. How lovely will our feet be when we bring the good news of God's peace and salvation everywhere we walk.

The gold jewelry and crowned headdress

This wardrobe just keeps getting better and better! Men have expressed their love and value for women by the jewelry they adorn them with since the beginning of time. No other part of your wardrobe expresses the value God has for you more than the jewels He adorns Israel (the church) with in Ezekiel 16:11-12 NKJV: "I adorned you with ornaments, put bracelets on your wrists, and a chain on your neck. And I put a jewel in your nose, earrings in your ears, and a beautiful crown on your head." God dresses you in jewels because He wants you to rule and reign with Him as His beloved bride (Ephesians 1:22-23; 2:6).

But wait—there is so much more to this verse. Another reason God dresses you in this headdress is because Isaiah explained that Jesus, "the Lord of hosts shall become a crown of glory and a diadem of beauty to the [converted] remnant of His people" (Isaiah 28:5). Jesus is our glorious crown. God has adorned us with Jesus. But there is even more.

Isaiah 62:3 AMP says: "You shall also be [so beautiful and prosperous as to be thought of as] a crown of glory and honor in the hand of the Lord, and a royal diadem [exceedingly beautiful] in the hand of your God." Just as Jesus is your crown, you are His crown too. It is such a beautiful picture of the marriage of the Lord and His bride which exemplifies the reciprocity God longs to have with us in our fellowship with Him.

John Gill (1697-1771), English Baptist pastor, biblical scholar, and theologian, in his Exposition of the Bible comments:

"The church and her members are glorious in themselves, through the righteousness of Christ put upon them;...they are regarded by him as a crown is by a prince; as a crown of massy gold, stuck with jewels, is rich and valuable, so are they in the eyes of Christ; they are dear and precious to him; high in his esteem; which he will not suffer to be trampled upon, or to be taken away from him, no more than a prince will suffer his crown to be so used or lost..."[33]

While reading Gill's wonderful commentaries on the crown, I was reminded of Watchman Nee's story of visiting George Cutting, the writer of the old, well-known paper tract Safety, Certainty and Enjoyment:

"When I was ushered into the presence of this old saint of ninety-three years, he took my hand in his and in a quiet, deliberate way he said: "Brother, do you know, I cannot do without him? And do you know, he cannot do without me? Though I was with him for over an hour, his great age and physical frailty made any sustained conversation impossible. But what remains in my memory of that interview was his frequent repetition of these two questions: "Brother, do you know, I cannot do without him? And do you know he cannot do without me?"[34]

We cannot do without God and He cannot do without us. When the prodigal son returned, it was the father who went running out to meet him and was just as thrilled to have him back as the son was to come home. As Jesus told the parable about the rich man selling all He had to buy the pearl of great price (Matt 13:45-46), *you* are the pearl of great price and Jesus gave all He had (His life) to purchase you. God wants you to be His beautiful shining diamond beauty dressed in a royal wardrobe to reflect His value for you as His bride and "jewel of great price." Therefore, He will adorn you with jewels representing what you are to Him and who He is to you.

You have now been beautifully decked from head to toe with love and grace in this ensemble fit for the Bride of the living God. You can carry these things He has given you as tools to strengthen, protect, and minister, living out God's perfect plan as a representation of His light and beauty from the inside out. But the journey does not end here, just as your day does not end when you finish getting ready in the morning and exit the bathroom. God will continue to beautify you, strengthen

CHAPTER EIGHT

you, and make your diamond beauty stronger, brighter and bigger every time you invite Him in to carry out His perfect plan, making you into His crowning jewel. A diamond fit for the King.

Conclusion

Dear Sister,

    We've come to the end of the beauty road together. It has been an honor and a blessing for me to share the things God has spoken to my heart about His desire to make you beautiful from the inside-out. As I have prayed for how to end this book, a simple letter sharing my heart and prayer for you seemed best. My heart for you is that you have a desire to reach and press on for diamond beauty with all your heart for the rest of your life (Philippians 3:14). I know God cherishes you and wants you to be beautiful His way because it is the only way that has lasting eternal value through His plan of salvation.

My earnest prayer is that you will not just settle for the world's beauty plan, but that you will become washed by the Word, radiant in holiness, and arrayed in the fine linen dress of your righteous acts as God's special jewel. I pray that you will take time to dine with the Lord daily, letting him fill you with His strength (Psalm 23:5).

I am fully confident that as you follow God's plan and let Him transform you into that brilliant, unconquerable "shining light" (Philippians 2:15), you will become a living, breathing reflection of God's glory in this world, a woman whose worth is "far above rubies" (Proverbs 31:10) because "He who promised is faithful" (Hebrews 10:23). May you walk in the richness of your inheritance in Christ being filled to the full by Him who fills all in all. Amen.

Your sister in Him,

Dona

Reflection Questions

INTRODUCTION AND CHAPTER ONE:

1. What is the purpose and goal of God's beautification process? Read Psalm 8:5, Isa 60:1-2, Ezekiel 16:14.

   a) Ephesians 2:10 describes us as God's _____. This is the Greek word _____ which literally means we are designed to be God's _____ _____ _____.

   b) Psalm 84:1 and Ephesians 2:22 says we are beautiful because we are God's _____ _____.

   c) Have you thought of yourself in these ways before? How does it change your self-concept to view your worth through what God says about you in the above verses?

2. Read Psalm 33:15; Psalm 139:13-18. What do these passages say about you as God's work of art?

3. Read Ezekiel 16:7-14. List the ways God cares for His bride in these verses. Do you believe God cares for you in these ways? If so, how does He express it in your life?

4. What are the ways God has made you individually beautiful? What fears and doubts came up for you during that question?

(If you're leading a group, pause and pray for all the items identified here so the group can pull down any strongholds each woman may be struggling with.)

Let's Pray

God, Help my thoughts and perceptions about myself to line up with the truth of Your Word. I declare that you want me to be beautiful in every way. Please search my heart and show me the ways I do not believe you in this area of my life. Heal me and change me in any way that I need it. Make me a living, breathing, expression of your Glory. Amen.

Chapter 2:

1. Define the Inside-Out Plan:

   a) What negative emotions does God replace with power, love and a sound mind according to 2 Tim 1:7, John 14:27, 1 John 4:18?

   b) How does replacing the feeling of fear with a sound mind help you to develop diamond beauty from the inside out?

2. a) How do we develop sound judgment according to 2Tim 1:13, 3:14,15?

   b) What do these verses tell you about the value of hearing the Word of God? Rev. 1:3, Acts 17:11?

3. What are the results of us "holding fast" what we hear in 2Tim. 3:15 and 17?

4. As you read the following scriptures, ask yourself what the connection is between our thoughts, words, and health? Proverbs 15:30; 16:23,24; 17:22 and Luke 6:45?

5. Take a moment now and examine your heart: Are there any negative thoughts you meditate on that rob you of peace? Do you have thoughts that you know you need to ask the Holy Spirit to help you demolish about yourself? Pick one scripture from this study guide that

stuck out to you to "hold fast" this week to help walk in a sound mind.

Let's Pray

Lord, I give you my mind, heart and body. I give them to you to transform and beautify into Your image and glory. Convict me, Holy Spirit, to turn my mind and heart to meditate on whatever is pure, and holy and of good report so I can grow in power, and love and develop a sound mind. Amen.

CHAPTER 3:

1. Define salvation: _____.

2. Read Psalm 103:1-5 and list the 5 benefits of salvation that restore us inside and out:

3. The key attitude to be beautified with salvation is humility or meekness. Read Psalm 37:11, Prov. 22:4, and Matt 5:5. What rewards shall God give the humble?

How was Jesus an example of humility to us? Read Matt. 21:5 and Phil 2:7-9.

5. In Exodus 33:19; 34:6, Psalm 103:11-14, and Matthew 18:27 what attribute of God makes Him forgiving of our sins?

6. How does persisting in sin make prayer for healing impossible? Read Psalm 66:18, Isa.1:15, 16; 59:1,2, Micah 3:4.

7. What does Hebrews 5:7, 8; 12:2, and 1Peter 4:1,2 say will be the benefits of suffering for God's servants?

8. What do the following passages tell us about God's lovingkindness: Psalm 40:11, Psalm 42:8, Psalm 51:1, Psalm 89:33, Psalm 119:88, 149, 159?

9. According to Psalm 103:5 and Isaiah 40:31 what is a characteristic of those that look to the Lord for their strength?

10. Take a moment now and examine your heart: Which benefit of salvation are you most thankful for? Why?

Let's Pray

Lord, thank you for forgiving me, healing me, saving me from destruction. I am so grateful for Your loving-kindness and mercy. Lord, I open my mouth wide to receive all the good things you feed me with from your Word. Renew me and strengthen me. Amen.

CHAPTER 4:

1. In John 10:10 and 1Peter 5:8 what is the goal of the devil in people's lives?

2. Define deception:

3. Read Romans 14 and 15:1-6. What should our attitude be to Christians who have different personal standards of holiness according to verses 14:1-3, 10, and 13?

In 15:1-3 what does Paul say we should do to build and edify another brother who has different personal standards?

4. Read Isaiah 53:3-5, Hebrews 4:15. How can Jesus relate to abuse by others? To us in our weaknesses?

5. According to Matt 5:43-48 and Romans 12:18-21 what is the way Jesus calls us to handle the hurts and abuse we endure?

6. Read Psalm 73:18-20, 27. What is the end for people who trust in the power of their beauty or fame rather than God?

7. According to Proverbs 31:28-31 what is the end for a woman who fears the Lord?

8. Take a moment now and examine your heart: Are there any ways you have allowed your attitudes or desires for beauty to be conformed to this world's mindsets? How? Lay them down on the altar before the Lord and ask Him to transform your mind and understanding.

Let's Pray

Lord, open the understanding of my mind and heart to embrace Your standards and plan for my beauty rather than the world's. Help me not to be deceived or conformed to settle for less than You have for me. Hold me by my right hand and guide me with Your counsel. Be the strength of my heart and my portion forever. Amen.

CHAPTER 5:

1. Water baptism is a fundamental Church practice found in the New Testament. What has been your experience with it? Write down some of your thoughts about your understanding and its significance for you. Read Romans 6:3-7, Galatians 3:27, Colossians 2:12 to help.

2. Read Psalm 119:9, 11, 105, 142, 151; John 15:3, Romans 10:17 and Ephesians 5: 26. What are some purposes for God's Word in our lives?

3. According to Hebrews 4:12, how does God's Word accomplish changing us? Have you had this experience after reading, meditating or applying a scripture in your life?

4. What are some of God's promises if we stay on the Highway of Holiness? Read Proverbs 3:5,6; 16:17; Isaiah 35:8-10.

5. Answer the following questions about Ezekiel 47:

   a) In Ezekiel verse 1 God shows Ezekiel the source of the healing water. What was it? What does this mean to you?

   b) How was Ezekiel directed to enter the water in verses 3, 4, 5? What can you conclude about our relationship with God and our understanding of the "water" of His Word based on this?

c) Where were the waters flowing and what happened when they got there in verses 8 and 9?

d) In verse 12 and Psalm 1:1-3, Jeremiah 17:7-8 what are the characteristics of the trees that live by the river? How do they get so prosperous? Does this relate to your life? How?

6. God's presence brings healing and refreshing. Read Psalm 16:11; 36:8,9; 46:4,5. What are the blessings associated with the river of God's presence in these verses?

7. Consider your heart: How much time do you spend daily with God in His Word and Presence? Is there any way you would like to change that? How?

Let's Pray

Lord, You are the Living Water. Fill me to overflowing because I am thirsty to know You and walk in Your ways. I want to get in the water more deeply than ever before. Take me to a place of healing and refreshing. Put a hunger in me like never before to read and understand your Word so I can be equipped and complete. Amen.

CHAPTER 6:

1. How will holiness make us a diamond beauty? What conclusions do you come to from Romans 8:29-30, Ephesians 5:27, Revelation 21:9-11?

2. a) How does holiness affect our relationship with God? Read Matthew 5:8, Psalm 29:2; 96:9.

> b) What are the results of a close relationship with God according to Psalm 16:11 and John 15:10-11?
>
> c) How does holiness affect our relationship to the world according to Lev. 20:23-26, 1 Thess.4:7-8?

3. How does God guide us to optimal functioning through holiness according to Acts 1:8, Ephesians 2:10 and 1 Timothy 2:21?

4. What are some reasons we go through the furnace of affliction according to Psalm 51:6-7, Malachi 3:2-3, Matthew 5:11-12, and 1Peter 1:6-7?

5. Why is the fear of the Lord a treasure? Read Proverbs 1:7, 3:13-18, Isaiah 33:6.

6. Consider your heart: Has your attitude toward holiness and affliction changed as a result of learning about its purpose and results in this chapter? How?

Let's Pray

God, search me and know my heart; try me and know my anxieties. See if there are any things in me that need to change. Purify my heart and mind so I can know the joy of walking with You in all Your ways. I want to be radiant in holiness, and sanctified so I can fulfill my purpose. Amen.

Chapter 7:

1. According to Psalm 23:5, God sets a table for us in the presence of our enemies. Who are the enemies that stop you from being the woman you want to be? How will feeding on God's "food" help you fight those enemies according to Psalm 34:8-10, Psalm 37:3-4, Psalm 103:5, and Isaiah 26:3-4?

2. Jesus is the bread of life. What is the value of Jesus' body and blood for us according to John 6:53-58? Was Jesus speaking literally according to John 6:63?

3. What pattern of eating God's word is set down in Exodus 16:4 and how can you reflect that in your own life?

4. Read Psalm 19:7-11. Why is God's word sweeter than honey?

5. What are the benefits of the oil of the Holy Spirit in these verses: Isaiah 61:3, Romans 15:13, 16, James 5:14, Mark 6:13?

6. The bread of idleness in Proverbs 31:27 AMP is gossip, discontent and self-pity:

   a) Read James 3:2-12 and explain what it says about the importance of the tongue.

b) Why can we be content no matter our circumstances according to Psalm 16:5-6?

c) How is Ephesians 1:18-20 contradictory to the feeling of self-pity?

7. Consider your heart: Think of a verse or two that you can feed on this week to help you fight your enemies more effectively. Write them down where you can see them throughout the week.

Let's Pray

Lord, thank you for the table you set for me. Draw my heart to come and sit with you and dine on your word during the times of the day I am attacked by my enemies so I can be in perfect peace. I will feed on your faithfulness. You anoint my head with oil; my cup runs over. I declare that surely goodness and mercy shall follow me all the days of my life (Psalm 23:5-6). Amen.

Chapter 8:

1. Why are the garments of salvation so costly?

2. What is the response of God's servants because of the way God dresses them? Read Psalm 30:11 and Psalm 132:16.

3. What does the linen dress represent according to Revelation 19:8?

4. According to Philippians 2:12-15 what is the motivation for these acts?

5. Read Isaiah 30:15 and 1 Peter 3:4. What makes a woman strong according to these verses? Explain.

6. A. How do we have peace according to Romans 14:19, Hebrews 12:14, and 1 Peter 3:10-11? How do we pursue it according to Ephesians 6:15?

7. Isaiah 52:7 tells us how to walk in our gospel shoes. What should we be proclaiming to others?

8. How does our crown represent salvation according to Isa. 28:5 and Eph. 6:17?

9. Reading Zechariah 9:16 and Isaiah 62:3, you are Jesus' crown just as much as He is yours. As His bride,

how does that relate to the model marriage plan in your opinion?

10. Consider your heart: Has your estimation of your value to God based on his garments of salvation changed? How?

Let's Pray

Lord, I shout aloud for joy because of your love and value for me. You have clothed me with the costly garments of salvation through your blood sacrifice. You are worthy of all my glory, and honor. Let my life be a sacrifice of praise that gives glory to your name. Give me the grace and obedience to honor you in every action I take. Amen.

Acknowledgments

It truly takes a village to write a book. I want to thank the following people for being a part of my village:

My daughter Charis who spent many afternoons reading, encouraging, and making great editing changes to my original manuscript. I can't even begin to tell you what an encouragement you have been to me. You wouldn't let me give up when I wanted to walk away. You believed in this book when I wasn't sure. This book would not have been completed without you.

My husband, Jim, and my amazing kids, Sage, Heather, Jared, and Rachel who always support and encourage me to follow my dreams and the path God leads me to. You are the joys of my life.

Katie Ryan, Alexa Beechler, Theresa Mack, Leela Harris, Erin Kiu, Raechelle Rodriguez, Jeena Thevathasan, Sue Kennedy, Alisa DiLorenzo, and Jen Cortes who pray with me, study God's word with me and prophesy hope and life into me. You are my personal "great company of witnesses" who have regularly inspired me to keep writing and fulfilling God's plan for me.

The wonderful Tim and Kristin Runyan who opened up the "Runyan Writers Retreat" at a moment's notice, and kept the tea and coffee flowing, so I could complete the final draft of the book. I appreciate your example of what true kindness and hospitality look like.

About the Author

With her combined background in teaching, pastoral work and counseling, Dona Moriarty has over 26 years of experience helping others grow, heal, and change. After years of watching women and teen girls, who would come to her counseling office, struggle with their beauty and appearance, and tired of being caught up in the exhaustion of chasing fading body perfection in her own life, Dona began to pray that God would show her His beauty plan for women. If beauty was one of God's blessings for women, she wanted to walk in it – God's way. Dona lives in Poway, California with her beautiful family.

If you enjoyed this book, please leave a review to help women like you receive this message!

You can find Dona on Instagram at @dona.moriarty

Chapter References

Introduction:

1. Brittany Irvine, "12 Surprising Statistics about the Beauty Industry," StyleCaster, August 29, 2013, https://stylecaster.com/beauty/surprising-statistics-beauty-industry.

2. National Eating Disorders Association Fact Sheet (May 2008). http://www.nationaleatingdisorders.org/uploads/file/in-the-news/NEDA-In-the-NewsFact-Sheet.pdf

3. Hoovers.com. "Cosmetics, Beauty Supply and Perfume Stores Industry Overview." http://www.hoovers.com/cosmetics,-beauty-supply,-and-perfume-stores/--ID__294--/ free-ind-fr-profile-basic.xhtml

4. Jessica Bennett, "Are We Turning Tweens into 'Generation Diva'?," Newsweek, March 29, 2009, https://www.newsweek.com/are-we-turning-tweens-generation-diva-76425.

5. Jessica Bennett, "Are We Turning Tweens into 'Generation Diva'?," Newsweek, March 29, 2009, https://www.newsweek.com/are-we-turning-tweens-generation-diva-76425.

6. "Homepage," The Aesthetic Society, accessed April 8, 2023, http://www.surgery.org/public/consumer/trends/new-study-suggests-young-adults-more-approving-of-cosmetic-surgery.

7. Jessica Bennett, "Are We Turning Tweens into 'Generation Diva'?," Newsweek, March 29, 2009, https://www.newsweek.com/are-we-turning-tweens-generation-diva-76425.

8. "DiamondOnNet: Wholesale Loose Diamonds and Diamond Engagement Rings," www.diamondonnet.com, n.d., https://www.diamondonnet.com/knowledges?page=2.

Chapter 1:

9. Andrew B Newberg and Mark Robert Waldman, How God Changes Your Brain: Breakthrough Findings from a Leading Neuroscientist (New York: Ballantine Books Trade Paperbacks, 2010).

Chapter 2:

10. "US Depression Rate," USAFacts, accessed April 8, 2023, https://usafacts.org/data/topics/people-society/health/health-risk-factors/depression/?utm_source=bing&utm_medium=cpc&utm_campaign=ND-

StatsData&msclkid=befaaaf8fd241a1b22c6c98a6815ec02.

11. Jack W Hayford et al., New Spirit-Filled Life Bible (Nelson Bibles, 2006).

12. Dictionary.com. "Dictionary.com | Meanings & Definitions of English Words," 2023. https://www.dictionary.com/.

13. Jerry Bridges, The Practice of Godliness (Colorado Springs: Navpress, 2016).

14. Healthy Living. "Signs & Symptoms of High Uric Acid Levels," 2017. https://healthyliving.azcentral.com/signs-symptoms-of-high-uric-acid-levels-12298602.html.

15. "It's National Sleep Day! 8 New Findings about Sleep and Your Health," HuffPost, January 3, 2013, http://www.huffingtonpost.com/2013/01/03/national-sleep-day-new-sleep-research-findings_n_2398403.html#slide=1938616.

Chapter 3:

16. Dictionary.com. "Dictionary.com | Meanings & Definitions of English Words," 2023. https://www.dictionary.com/.

17. "Lovingkindness-Definition of Hesed | Precept Austin," www.preceptaustin.org, June 6, 2022, http://preceptaustin.org/lovingkindness-definition_of_hesed.htm.

Chapter 4:

18. "Bing," https://www.bing.com/.

Chapter 6:

19. Michael Kerr, "Depression in the LGBTQIA+ Population," Healthline, March 29, 2012, https://www.healthline.com/health/depression/gay.

20. "Consecrate - Bible Meaning & Definition - Baker's Dictionary," biblestudytools.com, accessed April 8, 2023, http://www.biblestudytools.com/dictionaries/bakers-evangelical-dictionary/consecrate.html.

21. "Sanctification - Bible Meaning & Definition - Baker's Dictionary," biblestudytools.com, accessed April 8, 2023, http://www.biblestudytools.com/dictionaries/bakers-evangelical-dictionary/sanctification.html.

22. Hobart M King, "Diamond: A Gem Mineral with Properties for Industrial Use," Geology.com, 2018, http://geology.com/minerals/diamond.shtml.

23. "DiamondOnNet: Wholesale Loose Diamonds and Diamond Engagement Rings," www.diamondonnet.com, accessed April 9, 2023, https://www.diamondonnet.com/knowledges?page=3.

24. Jerry Bridges, The Pursuit of Holiness (Colorado Springs, Colorado: Navpress, 2016).

Chapter 7:

25. "Honey - Meaning and Verses in Bible Encyclopedia," biblestudytools.com, accessed April 8, 2023, http://www.biblestudytools.com/encyclopedias/isbe/honey.html.

26. "HelpGuide.org," https://www.helpguide.org, accessed April 8, 2023, http://www.helpguide.org/life/healthy_diet_fats.htm#types.

27. "Incomplete vs. Complete Proteins / Nutrition / Proteins," www.fitday.com, accessed April 8, 2023, http://www.fitday.com/fitness-articles/nutrition/proteins/incomplete-vs-complete-proteins.html.

28. "Oil - Bible Meaning & Definition - Baker's Dictionary," biblestudytools.com, accessed April 8, 2023,

http://www.biblestudytools.com/dictionaries/bakers-evangelical-dictionary/oil.html.

29. http://www.answers.com/topic/discontent

30. http://www.urbandictionary.com/define.php?term=Self-pity

31. Thomas à Kempis, The Imitation of Christ (Peabody: Hendrickson Publishers, 2004).

32. "HelpGuide.org," https://www.helpguide.org, accessed April 8, 2023, http://www.helpguide.org/life/healthy_diet_fats.htm#types.

Chapter 8:

33. "Isaiah 62 Commentary - John Gill's Exposition of the Bible," biblestudytools.com, accessed April 8, 2023, http://www.biblestudytools.com/commentaries/gills-exposition-of-the-bible/isaiah-62/.

34. Watchman Nee, The Normal Christian Life. (Tyndale House, 1977).

Additional Sources

Anonymous. The Cloud of Unknowing Anonymous. Createspace Independent Publishing Platform, 2017.

Answers. "Answers - the Most Trusted Place for Answering Life's Questions," n.d. http://www.answers.com/topic/discontent.

Bonhoeffer, Dietrich. The Cost of Discipleship. New York: Simon & Schuster, 1995.

Bridges, Jerry. The Practice of Godliness. Colorado Springs: Navpress, 2016.

Bridges, Jerry. The Pursuit of Holiness. Colorado Springs, Colorado: Navpress, 2016.

GrrlScientist. "Mystery Bird: Rüppell's Griffon Vulture, Gyps Rueppellii." The Guardian, March 5, 2011, sec. Science. http://www.guardian.co.uk/science/punctuated-equilibrium/2011/mar/05/5.

Hayford, Jack W. New Spirit Filled Life Bible. Nashville, Tennessee: Thomas Nelson Publishers, 2013.

Kempis, Thomas à. The Imitation of Christ. Peabody: Hendrickson Publishers, 2004.

King, Hobart M. "Diamond: A Gem Mineral with Properties for Industrial Use." Geology.com, 2018. http://geology.com/minerals/diamond.shtml.

Lawrence, Brother. The Practice of the Presence of God: With Spiritual Maxims. Grand Rapids, Michigan: Spire Books, 1967.

Nee, Watchman. The Normal Christian Life. Tyndale House, 1977.

Newberg, Andrew B, and Mark Robert Waldman. How God Changes Your Brain: Breakthrough Findings from a Leading Neuroscientist. New York: Ballantine Books Trade Paperbacks, 2010.

Orr, James, M.A., D.D. General Editor. "Entry for 'HONEY'". "International Standard Bible Encyclopedia". 1915.

Taylor, Howard, and Geraldine Taylor. Hudson Taylor's Spiritual Secret. Chicago: Moody Publishers, 2009.

Tozer, A W. The Crucified Life. Gospel Light Publications, 2011.

Tyndale House Publishers. Holy Bible: New Living Translation. Wheaton, Ill.: Tyndale House Publishers, 2004.

www.biblegateway.com. "Amplified Bible (AMP) - Version Information - BibleGateway.com." Accessed April 8, 2023.

http://www.biblegateway.com/versions/Amplified-Bible-AMP.

www.biblestudytools.com. "Psalm 132:16 Commentary - the Treasury of David." http://www.biblestudytools.com/commentaries/treasury-of-david/psalms-132-16.html.

www.biblestudytools.com. "Baker's Evangelical Dictionary of Biblical Theology." http://www.biblestudytools.com/dictionaries/bakers-evangelical-dictionary.

www.biblestudytools.com. "Honey - Meaning and Verses in Bible Encyclopedia." http://www.biblestudytools.com/encyclopedias/isbe/honey.html.

www.diamondonnet.com. "DiamondOnNet: Wholesale Loose Diamonds and Diamond Engagement Rings," n.d. https://www.diamondonnet.com/knowledges.

www.Dictionary.com. "Dictionary.com | Meanings & Definitions of English Words," 2023. https://www.dictionary.com/.

www.fitday.com. "Incomplete vs. Complete Proteins / Nutrition / Proteins.". http://www.fitday.com/fitness-articles/nutrition/proteins/incomplete-vs-complete-proteins.html.

www.helpguide.org. "HelpGuide.org." http://www.helpguide.org/life/healthy_diet_fats.htm#types.

The Holy Spirit. "Baptism in the Holy Spirit." https://theholyspirit.com/study-series/baptism-in-the-holy-spirit/.

www.preceptaustin.org. "Lovingkindness-Definition of Hesed | Precept Austin," June 6, 2022. http://preceptaustin.org/lovingkindness-definition_of_hesed.htm.

Urban Dictionary. "Urban Dictionary: Self-Pity." Accessed April 9, 2023. http://www.urbandictionary.com/define.php?term=Self-pity.

Wikipedia. "Diamond," April 6, 2023. http://en.wikipedia.org/wiki/Diamond.

Made in the USA
Monee, IL
26 September 2023